Conversation Skills Training:
How to Build Relationships, Navigate Any Situation, and Talk to Anyone

By Patrick King
Social Interaction and Conversation Coach at
www.PatrickKingConsulting.com

Table of Contents

CHAPTER 1. THE BASICS ARE NOT SO BASIC — 7

- IDENTIFY YOUR COMMUNICATION STYLE — 8
- PSYCHOLOGICAL BARRIERS TO COMMUNICATION — 22
- THE RAPPORT GAME — 42
- EXPRESSING WITHOUT SPEAKING — 56

CHAPTER 2. TOOLS OF THE CHARMING — 73

- HAVE BETTER CONVERSATIONS WITH THE RULE OF THREE — 73
- SUSTAIN CONVERSATIONS WITH CONVERSATIONAL THREADING AND USEFUL ACRONYMS — 83
- USEFUL CONVERSATIONAL ACRONYMS — 90

CHAPTER 3. EQ > IQ — 97

- VALIDATION AS CONNECTION — 109
- ACCEPTANCE AND THE SIX LEVELS OF LISTENING — 122

CHAPTER 4. AS IF IT WASN'T HARD ENOUGH… — 137

- HOW TO SAY NO — 148
- HOW TO COMMUNICATE WHEN YOU DON'T AGREE — 154

THE SIX-STEP APOLOGY — 171

CHAPTER 5. GOAL-ORIENTED COMMUNICATION — 183

HOW TO PERSUADE ANYONE — 183
THE OFFICE. — 195

SUMMARY GUIDE — 211

Chapter 1. The Basics Are Not So Basic

Communication is *everything*. No matter who you are or what you are trying to achieve in your life, improving your communication skills is a must. It's a strange fact that human beings are expected to just know how to communicate—despite so many of us finding it challenging or unpleasant! The truth is that good communication takes time, effort, and know-how. It follows known principles and laws. Luckily, being a charismatic speaker, empathetic listener, and skillful negotiator and mediator is not something reserved for the select few—it's something that anyone can do if only you understand these laws.

There is certainly not enough space in just one book to cover all the multifaceted ways that communication can be finetuned and tweaked. But in the following chapters, we're going to explore some of the most popular concepts and principles so you feel empowered to start making positive changes right now. One idea that we will return to frequently is the overall *purpose* of communication. We reach out to one another to connect, to meet our needs, to express ourselves, and to solve problems. **Therefore, the best mindset to adopt on our mission to become better communicators is the one that will best allow us to do just that: connect.**

Identify Your Communication Style

When learning how to communicate better, **it's important to understand your exact starting point, i.e., how good is your communication ability currently?** If you've picked up this book, chances are there are some aspects of the way you communicate that you've identified as needing improvement.

But communication is not just one skill, but a complex mix of many. On top of that, there are different *styles* of communication. Even if you don't consider yourself a good communicator currently, you have a unique and characteristic type of communication whether you're conscious of it or not. As we move through the chapters of this book, we'll be looking at concrete ways to consciously choose the best and most effective styles of communication rather than default to unconscious patterns that may not really be working for us.

When you can communicate well, your relationships take on an extra dimension of quality and intimacy, you find yourself in conflict far less often, and you give yourself the gift of being seen and understood so that other people have the best possible chance of meeting your needs. But without good communication, everything—relationships, work, conflict resolution—becomes much, much harder, if not impossible.

Before we learn the best ways to communicate, let's ask ourselves: how do we communicate right now? Take a look at the following communication style profiles and see if you can recognize yourself in one (or more!) of them:

The Passive Communicator

For this kind of communicator, it's all about what isn't said. **Passive communication avoids expressing needs and wants, avoids conflict, and doesn't directly and obviously convey thoughts or feelings**. Imagine two friends going out for a drink. The first asks the second where he'd like to go, the second says, "Oh, I don't mind. You choose somewhere."

The first does choose somewhere, and the second doesn't actually like it . . . but doesn't say so. Instead, he gets quietly annoyed and resentful. When the first friend asks what's wrong, the second says, "Oh, nothing, I'm fine," while very obviously *not* being fine!

At the end of the evening, things come to a head and the passive friend has an emotional outburst, snapping rudely. Immediately, he apologizes and acts submissive and guilty. He goes home wondering how he keeps ending up in such emotionally fraught situations when he works so hard to avoid confrontation. Sound familiar? You might have a passive communication style.

People who communicate this way may have learned in early childhood experiences that it is not possible to ever express their feelings directly, or that they may as well not ask for what they want since they have no real chance of getting it. Think of it this way: A passive communication style usually exists because, at some point and in some way, it works. However, it usually creates more problems in the long run, and if you've ever dealt with a passive communicator, you'll know that it actually undermines how much genuine connection there can be. If you suspect this is your default communication mode, take a look at some other clues:

- You apologize for expressing yourself or sharing your (perfectly reasonable) wants and needs
- You find it difficult to make decisions, lead, or take responsibility

- You sometimes feel like a victim or like others dominate you
- You often prefer to opt out or let others take control
- You're indecisive, preferring others to make all the plans
- You sometimes don't know what you really think or feel
- You tend to blame others for bad things that happen
- You don't generally feel in control of situations, or your life generally

Nonverbally, passive communicators tend to speak quietly and adopt a small, submissive posture, or else fidget nervously or avoid eye contact. The irony is that a passive communicator does not achieve the result they want with this behavior. Other people can feel frustrated, guilty, exasperated, or annoyed with you, or else they may see the passivity as an invitation to take advantage. On the other hand, a passive communicator can leave others feeling unwilling to help anymore since their efforts are often met with a passive, defeatist attitude that lacks energy and autonomy.

The Aggressive Communicator

Where the passive communicator expresses too little of their needs and wants, the aggressive communicator goes too far in the other direction. **They know what they want, and they will be as demanding, intimidating, and even hostile as they need to be to get it.**

From this point of view, communication is a war, and the aggressive communicator is one who intends to win and beat down their opponent. This can be that office bully who is always loud, threatening, and abrasive, but it doesn't always have to be as blatant as this. Sometimes, the one person in a family or friend group whom everyone is most afraid of is the one who is simply unpredictable.

Imagine a family is out at a restaurant and the toddler is trying to catch the attention of two adults who are speaking. The toddler wants to communicate the message "listen to me," and they end up doing it by banging on the table, raising their voice, getting angry, and squirming around in their seat, threatening to topple glasses on the table. The result is that everyone immediately turns their attention to the child. This is the power of aggressive communication—it makes people pay attention and respond quickly! You can also see the disadvantage of this communication style, though: People may give you what you want, but if you're behaving like a toddler to get it, they may well resent you in the process.

An aggressive communicator might literally yell and scream, saying "Don't be stupid!" or scoffing loudly at what you say, but they can also be aggressive in their body language or actions:

- Sharp, sudden, or "big" gestures
- Hogging space
- Towering over others
- Scowling, glaring, frowning
- Invading people's personal space
- "My way or the highway" attitude

Again, the result is ironic: Most people might comply with an aggressive communicator, at least at first, but they quickly can grow defensive, uncooperative, and resentful. Nobody likes to be humiliated or hurt, and so the result is often less respect but more defensiveness and pushback—the last thing an aggressive communicator actually wants.

If this kind of communication seems like your style, don't be too hard on yourself. Again, learning to express yourself this way often comes down to faulty learning experiences in childhood and can point to feelings of fear, powerlessness, and frustration. Find more nuanced ways of expressing your needs, and you'll realize you can get what you want without drama or force!

The Passive-Aggressive Communicator

We all know someone like this! This style of communication is as aggressive as the previous one, only it's covert, i.e., hidden and indirect. Things are not what they seem on the surface. **Someone who communicates this way may feel angry but powerless to act in direct or ordinary ways—so they attempt to meet their needs and make themselves known passively instead**. If you've grown up in an environment with other passive-aggressive communicators, it can be hard to be heard and stand your ground without resorting to the same tactics.

Passive-aggressive communicators may use heaps of sarcasm, they may complain bitterly and make a nuisance of themselves (without doing a thing to help themselves), or they may sulk until someone is forced to do something about it.

Otherwise, they may gossip, issue false apologies, or give compliments that are actually insults in disguise. They may engage in "malicious compliance" ("I will give the appearance of cooperation but actually not be compliant at all") or be difficult or unreliable instead of saying outright that they don't want to do something. There is a devious, almost two-faced feeling to this type of communication that leaves other people feeling manipulated, exhausted, or confused.

Imagine our two friends are out for a drink, and the passive one says, "Oh, you can choose a place. I don't mind." Let's say the other one has a passive-aggressive communication style, and although they resent being forced to make decisions all the time, they don't feel able to come out and say that directly.

So instead, they say, "Oh no, I understand. How could I forget that it's always my job to sort these things out, right?" As they deliver with a sugary-sweet smile, there is plausible deniability in this, and when the other friend responds to the hidden aggression in it, the first one can act hurt and confused: "Calm down . . . It was just a joke!" If pushed, the passive-aggressive friend may then apologize, but it will be an "apology" with a sting in the tail: "Sheesh, I said I'm sorry. Forgive me for not being perfect all the time . . ."

The Manipulative Communicator

The above style has some overlap with one more style, that of the manipulative communicator. This is the person who uses cunning and fakery to get what they want. **Manipulation is essentially a conscious attempt to control other people and have them do, say, and think as you'd like them to.** While the passive-aggressive communicator can hurt others indirectly in an attempt to express their needs without really expressing them, the manipulator is characterized by their ability to see others as tools, i.e., a means to an end. Understandably, this is one of the worst approaches and most likely to backfire.

A manipulative communicator might cry "crocodile tears" in order to make the other person feel sorry for them (instead of, for comparison, simply sharing their genuine experience and the other person responding with genuine, uncoerced empathy!). They may "ask without asking" or use emotional levers such as guilt and obligation to position people in ways that suit them. The woman who tells her husband, "Oh, I love how comfortable you are with being an underachiever. It's really inspiring how you don't care what other people think of you," is being manipulative if she knows that this will push him to take a higher-paying job that she wants him to take.

A manipulative communicator might see someone enjoying their lunch at work and say, seemingly to no one in particular in a high-pitched, condescending voice, "Oh, that looks *delicious*. Aren't you lucky? I wish I could eat such fancy stuff like that for lunch every day. Oh well."

Manipulative communication can sometimes "work," but more often than not it is rightly perceived by others as artificial, condescending, and untrustworthy. If outright tricks and lies are used, the communication style can fail badly and the person not only fails to get what they want, but they shut off potential genuine avenues of connection and understanding—shooting themselves in the foot, basically.

Now, in reading about these four communication styles, you can probably see that you've been guilty of all of them at least at some point in your life. You can also probably see that they overlap one another and that the tactics in each style can vary in intensity. Few people use any single type exclusively in their communication, but it is worth asking honestly about patterns that you observe in yourself. There are countless shades and nuances possible when we think about how *not* to communicate. Ultimately, though, there's one thing to keep in mind: None of them really WORK.

In other words, **the above four communication styles are "bad" not because they use lies, passivity, or force, but rather because they don't achieve the main goal of communication.** Why do people communicate? There are only a few primary reasons:

- To get our needs met
- To share our experience and express who we are
- To solve problems
- To connect with another human being

The above communication styles are actually attempts to meet some or all of these goals.

Usually, however, they achieve the exact opposite result. While it can be fun to identify annoying communication patterns in others, there is more to be gained by honestly asking where *we* ourselves fall short of ideal communication patterns.

Do we have a tendency to be aggressive, passive, passive-aggressive, or manipulative? Or even all four? Perhaps we are passive in some situations, and in others, overly aggressive or manipulative. For many people, they can communicate well when they feel safe and happy, but when threatened or tired, they can revert to less-than-ideal communication tactics.

It helps to be aware of maladaptive communication strategies, but let's also look at how we can best communicate, i.e., how we can meet our needs, express ourselves, and solve problems in a way that actually works. The truth is that genuine, healthy, and respectful communication is just so much easier and more pleasant.

The Assertive Communicator

This is a healthy, balanced, and conscious way of communicating. **It's the ability to express needs, wants, thoughts, and feelings in a direct and assertive way without ever disrespecting or controlling the way others think or feel, controlling what they do, or**

undermining what they need. This is the communication style that comes from a healthy self-esteem paired with a healthy sense of respect and compassion for others.

Have you ever encountered somebody who just exuded a sense of *okayness*? They might have seemed perfectly relaxed, calm, and self-possessed, and after speaking to them, you felt that they were kind and friendly, but not that they were pushovers. They didn't seem flustered, inhibited, forceful, or shy, but neither did they seem arrogant and in-your-face. Chances are, this stable, comfortable feeling you felt in their presence was due to their communication style.

In non-verbal expression, such people are self-controlled, balanced, relaxed, open, and respectful—and that means respect for themselves and others. Because of this, other people trust and like them, and if they don't, at the very least they know where they stand. People do not feel obliged to take care of them or forced to do things they don't want to in order to appease them. In the company of a person who communicates this way, things are clear, direct, mature, respectful, and relaxed no matter the kind of conversation unfolding.

They can say, "You know what, to be honest, I don't really feel like going out drinking tonight. I'm in the mood to just get some takeout and relax at home. What do you think? We could still pick up a couple of beers . . ."

They can express their needs or desires clearly, directly, and politely ("Oh, wow, that looks amazing! Would you mind if I had a tiny taste?") and simply don't need to control others or get them to take care of them (for example, no fishing for compliments needed because you are happy and confident with your choices and don't need external validation for them). Finally, assertive communicators are flexible and can set healthy boundaries when necessary, but they can also be open, trusting, and vulnerable at other times.

The first thing to realize is that certain communication styles are simply not effective and will not get you the results you want. **How you communicate is a choice**. You can make the best choice when you consciously understand what you're doing and why it's not working . . . so you can choose something that *will* work.

Every endeavor to improve must begin with a level of self-awareness. There is no shame or blame in identifying the current limits and blind spots in your own communication style. The quality of our relationships with others comes down to the quality of our communication. And guess what? The quality of our communication comes down one hundred percent to *us* and what we consciously choose for ourselves.

For now, be curious about what isn't working for you communication-wise. Think back to conflicts or communication breakdowns in the past and see if you can identify some of these less-than-helpful styles in yourself, the other person . . . or both. Before we continue, consider the attitude that inspires a healthy and assertive communication style. Read the following sentiments. Do any seem particularly alien to you or difficult to agree with? This might be a clue to the aspects of assertive communication you could develop in yourself:

"All people are equally entitled to express themselves as long as they're respectful."

"I'm confident in who I am, and I like myself."

"I have choices."

"I take responsibility for getting my needs met."

"I am comfortable speaking honestly and clearly."

"I am calm, positive, and measured when dealing with others."

"I don't need to or want to control others—I am more interested in self-mastery."

"I like to seek compromise and balance."

"I value my rights immensely. I also wouldn't dream of infringing on someone else's rights."

"Nobody owes me anything."

In the interest of increasing self-awareness, ask yourself the following questions:

What is my main style of communication?

What aspect of assertive communication do I find most difficult?

What would I most like to improve about the way I communicate?

Another way to gain insight into your own communication blind spots is to become more aware of how other people communicate with you. When you talk to someone, pay close attention to how they express their needs, how they're making you feel, and how much you trust them. Pay attention to your overall relationship with this person and how their communication style impacts that. Then, make inferences to your own style—do *you* have any of those annoying habits? What works and how can you learn to do the same yourself?

Psychological Barriers to Communication

In the previous chapter, we began by exploring people's habitual communication styles, and how we might start to use self-awareness and observation of others to better establish non-verbal rapport—the first task in any conversation.

It might seem strange for a book on communication to say the following, but it's true: Good communication is a natural, normal human ability, and it's something that anyone can do with ease. You might then ask if that's the case, why are so many people so bad at communicating? The answer is that **communicating well is simple and easy, but we first need to remove the formidable barriers that stand in our way to doing so.** *This* is what can be difficult.

People are only able to communicate at the level that their inner psychological barriers allow them to. For example, if there are two people, and one person has amazing communication skills but the other is trapped in a core belief that conversations are battles they need to win, then the conversation will never move beyond this battle framework.

Basically, one's emotional state, beliefs, habits, personality, and general attitude to life are the ultimate limits to how well they are able to connect to and communicate with others. Certain psychological states will improve your ability to both send and receive a message, while others will undermine it.

With that in mind, what barriers are there, and how can we replace them with something more useful?

Assumptions

Assuming is simply coming to a conclusion you don't strictly have evidence for. It almost always leads to misunderstanding. Communication, after all, is about learning about the other person and their message. If we think we already know all there is to know, then why have a conversation at all, right?

Imagine that a boss doesn't give detailed instructions to a new employee because she assumes that the employee will already know how to do the task. The employee doesn't and so fails at the task. Here, the barrier of assumption has stepped in and prevented any real communication from happening, but it can also rear its head once communication is underway. If you've ever had an argument and both found yourselves saying things like, "But I thought you meant X!" then you likely were both guilty of making assumptions.

In conversations, it's so easy to assume that all the mental models, frameworks, systems of meanings, values, and definitions that we hold are neatly shared by other people. We forget that they have their own goals and interpretations of events, and they may have their own understanding that can be identical to ours, completely opposite, or anything in between.

How do we know what kind of world the person in front of us is actually inhabiting? Well, we communicate with them! And this means no assumptions.

Instead, ask questions. Pretend you are a reporter or documentary filmmaker or alien from outer space . . . or all three. Empty your mind of any preconceptions and don't guess. Ask the other person to tell you what they think and feel. Sometimes, with some topics, you'll need to confirm even this, because after all, we all use words and ideas in different ways. Think of someone asking someone else to marry them. That person says yes. But what exactly have they agreed to? How big is the overlap between their respective understanding of the word "marriage"?

Aggression and Anger

We've already seen that aggressive (or passive-aggressive) communication styles cause upset and don't even achieve the person's communication goals anyway. But for obvious reasons, anger, resentment, or even rage can be serious obstacles to effective communication. It's simple: To communicate, we have to make contact. We connect with someone else, and this requires us to let our guards down and become receptive and open to what the other person is sharing. If the other person is angry, they will come across as a threat—and why would you ever be receptive to a threat?

Most sane people will close off to aggression and disconnect in an effort to protect themselves. This means that if you are leading with anger, you are automatically creating a condition in which communicating *cannot take place.* Think about that: **You cannot communicate with a threat, real or perceived. You can only defend against it.** If you lead with anger, you can only expect defensiveness from the other person—and this gets you nowhere.

Imagine the sadly all-too-common example of trying to make a complaint on the phone or get a refund from a dodgy company. Yes, you're entitled to feel angry, but will that anger help you solve your problems any quicker? If you spend fifteen minutes yelling at the person on the other end of the line, it's just fifteen minutes you've wasted, and at the end of it, you'll probably still be at square one.

Instead, own your emotions. Feeling angry is not a problem; approaching someone else with hostility and aggression is. The alternative is not to force yourself to pretend to be calm. Rather, it's to own your feelings and identify them as belonging to you. Instead of blaming the other person or directing your emotion to them, hold that emotion as something that belongs to you only. Using "I" statements will mean you can say, "I feel so overwhelmed right now," instead of, "You're stressing me out!"

Preconceived Attitudes

Here is the question yet again: What is the point of communication? What is it for, ultimately?

The way you answer this question shows you the attitude you hold toward communication. For some people, conversations are a fight or a courtroom drama or a way to prove how "right" and worthy they are. For others, the point is to get their needs met or share and express or simply reach outside the limits of their own inner perception and connect with another human being.

Naturally, the attitude you have to conversations will depend on the beliefs you hold. These beliefs also include the habitual roles you've always assumed in conversation with others. Do you routinely show up as the therapist, comedian, drill sergeant? Are you always preaching and explaining, or do you repeatedly defer to others and let them lead?

None of these orientations are right or wrong in themselves. But if you are a) unaware that they are there in the first place or b) constantly communicating with people who don't share your attitude, then you can expect conflict and misunderstanding.

One especially big impediment to effective communication is negative self-image, or low confidence. This acts like a kind of filter in which every message you receive from the outside world can only ever be interpreted in a way that makes you look inferior. Most of us have never considered that low self-esteem can distort communication, but really, if low self-esteem is the inability to hear a message that paints us in a good light, then that's precisely what it does!

In a 1980 paper called "Perceptions of the Impact of Negatively Valued Physical Characteristics on Social Interaction," researchers Robert Kleck and Angelo Strenta set up a fascinating experiment. They told their participants they were investigating prejudices and biases toward those with facial scarring. The participants were given fake facial scars and sent out to do real job interviews, then asked to report their experiences.

Just before doing the interviews, however, the participants were told that the makeup artists needed to quickly touch up the scar—while secretly they removed it. On returning from the interviews, the participants all claimed to have been discriminated against. Because they were *expecting* discrimination, they interpreted everything that occurred in the interview as evidence for that conclusion. In other words, if one sees themselves as a victim, one can't help but suddenly perceive everything as an attack.

The participants would easily say that what they perceived was something in the interviewers. But what do you suppose the interviewers made of them? Chances are, they, too, could detect the preconceptions the interviewees were bringing to the table—perhaps even unconsciously playing along to confirm them.

Instead, practice compassion—for self and others. Really good conversation is supremely democratic. There are no winners and losers and no hierarchy. Take a deep breath and put yourself on an even keel with the other person. Try to shelve any ideas about who is playing what role, and compassionately encounter the person you find as you find them—your equal.

At the same time, be on guard for any deep-seated beliefs that have made you decide that you will be the loser in any interaction before it even happens. The subtle ways that your behavior will change when you have genuine and healthy self-belief can make all the difference in the world.

Fear

Aggression impedes communication because it puts the other person on the defensive. But if that person is already on the defensive, the conversation is already impacted. **Defensiveness is essentially putting up a wall. Trying to communicate through a wall is not easy, and it usually results in one thing: confusion and serious misunderstanding.** This is sometimes why fear and aggression can lead to communication breakdown; the more walls that are put up, the harder it is to hear one another, and in the confusion, more fear and anger are created, necessitating even more walls ...

A person who is fearful is not listening. They are not curious. They are not focusing on anything other than their own self-preservation, and this makes them a bad conversationalist on the most fundamental level. Have you noticed how, after watching a horror movie, the bedroom that seemed perfectly innocent yesterday now seems riddled with potentially frightening nooks and crannies?

If someone is fearful, their impulse will be to protect themselves or escape—and you cannot communicate to or from that position. Imagine someone in the middle of a severe panic attack—they may *literally* be unable to hear you. All they know is their own crushing panic, and you may as well not even exist for them. Fear can make us see things that aren't there and, in communication, can make us detect threats where there aren't any, so the person having the panic attack suddenly decides that you're to blame for how they feel! Fear narrows our focus inward, so we lose perspective and can no longer connect with our environment. Naturally, real connection will be stunted.

Instead, relax and be curious. One way to do this is simple: ask an open-ended question. You don't have to lower your walls entirely, but at least be curious about what's on the other side!

Inflexibility and Need for Control

When you get together with someone and have a conversation, anything can happen. The thread of the talk can go in any direction, and at any one moment, the words either person says could steer the thing in a completely novel and unexpected direction. And this is a good thing! When two people get together to communicate, there is a chance for them to co-create something that is bigger than the sum of both of them. But, this can only happen if both parties are willing to relinquish a little control and *let* the conversation flow as it will.

Being inflexible, closed-minded, or hungry for control mean that we enter any discussion with a fixed idea of what it should be ... therefore preventing it from becoming anything else. This shuts us off from listening, from learning, and from responding spontaneously in the moment as it unfolds. It also makes us very boring and predictable!

Imagine two people on a blind date. It soon becomes clear there is no chemistry, but rather than trying to force it, feeling awkward, or calling the entire evening off, both decide that they're still having a nice time, and why not go to the arcade, since they're out anyway and it'll be fun? Incidentally, nobody would be surprised if in ten years' time, this became a cute "how we met" story. Often things happen best when we let go of the idea of how we think they should happen!

Instead, be willing to be surprised. Let the other person lead, and be genuinely open to the idea that they may steer the conversation in a way you did not expect or prepare for. Everyone has something to teach you.

Judgment and Premature Evaluation

Have you ever found yourself rushing in a conversation? You hear someone talking, but internally, you think, "Yes, yes, I've heard that . . ." and you subtly try to move them along. Why? Sometimes, this kind of haste signals that we have been too quick to come to conclusions about what we're being told. As with making assumptions, we think we already understand everything there is to understand and no longer need to engage. As we dig deeper, this sometimes tells us that we have prematurely gone into judgment mode before really hearing the other person.

We all have preconceived notions in our heads. When someone talks, we might flit through our catalogue of notions and see which ones match closest—then grab ahold of *that* and stop listening to what the unique person in front of us is saying. **Judgment—even "positive" judgments, kill what is real and nuanced in the present moment.** We fail to see the other person and their message and instead substitute it with our *idea* of who they are and what they're saying. This is the root of prejudice and bias. If we are interacting with two-dimensional stereotypes of people and not real people, then our communication is always going to be lacking.

Psychologist: So it seems like you have a lot of resentment toward your mother.

Patient: Well, no, not really. But I do think something changed when my brother was born and—

Psychologist: So the problem is your brother?

In this exchange, the psychologist has already come to a conclusion, and they're not really interested in gathering any more data. They have a hammer (i.e., "everyone has an issue with at least one family member"), and they're going to look at everything like it's a nail.

Instead, cultivate wonder. This may be the hardest mindset shift of all, but to become a genuinely good communicator, you need to maintain a sense not just of curiosity or interest in another person, but of near-continuous awe at what a privilege it really is to step outside your own head for a moment and step into someone else's.

In the remainder of this book, we will take as a starting point the value that *communication is a way to create connection.* We label anything that gets in the way of this connection as a "psychological barrier" and work to remove it. Are there other barriers than the ones listed above? Definitely. We can point to an attitude of distraction and inattention, lack of trust, cross-cultural limitations, and even exhaustion as things that prevent people from properly connecting.

Whatever they are, though, with self-awareness and practice, we can work to lessen their impact on us.

Other Bad Communication Habits to Avoid

Maybe you read the previous descriptions of barriers to communication and thought it all sounded a little serious. Perhaps you are simply looking for ways to improve everyday conversation, and not necessarily become a master at juggling the deep and meaningful stuff. However, even if you are on the whole a flexible, open-minded, and non-judgmental communicator, you may *still* fall into the common habitual conversational traps that plague the best of us.

That's because the biggest barrier to excellent communication is all those small, mindless, and automatic acts that erode trust and connection. Granted, these conversational habits don't mean that you have psychological issues with prejudice or a deep-seated need for control. But in a way, knee-jerk habits like these are worse because they are usually invisible, unconscious, and may even be encouraged by your general environment. Before we take an earnest look at what we should be doing to become better communicators, let's explore a few more things *not* to do.

Human life is largely comprised of conversations. Every relationship, every human interaction, every job, everything at some point requires you to encounter and engage with another human being. And whether you fancy yourself a world-class communicator or would sooner send an email than deal with face-to-face discussion, chances are you have at least a few terrible communication habits that drive people nuts. Yes, even you!

No, the following habits won't cause major blowouts or serious miscommunication, and they're not the end of the world . . . but they're good low-hanging fruit to begin with as we embark on sharpening our communication skills.

Constantly Interrupting

Maybe you interrupt because you're so excited by what the other person just said, you simply have to interject and say your thing. Maybe you interrupt because unconsciously, you think that what you have to say is more urgent or more important. Maybe, you're doing it because you're rushing the conversation along, having already jumped to conclusions about what the other person means and made your judgments about it.

In any case, it doesn't matter *why* you do it—only that it makes the other person feel awful. It's understandable—you want to be heard. But so do they! Take it a step further and don't even think about interrupting. You know what this means—when you are suddenly more interested in your own response to what's being said than listening to what's being said, it shows. The other person can tell that your attention has suddenly moved inward and you are preparing a response.

A good habit is this: After someone stops speaking, pause and count slowly to three in your head. This sends the message, "I'm here, I'm paying attention, and I care about what you have to say," and lets the other person know they don't have to rush to get a word in, and that you are respectful enough to pause to process what they're saying.

Multitasking

A conversation merits more than the few glances you can muster when you finally tear your eyes away from your iPhone. We are probably all guilty of the practice of multitasking at least occasionally. No matter how insignificant or pointless your interactions may appear, you must be there for them. In other words, you can't mindlessly check your phone or run through your grocery list. Pay close attention to the people you're talking to.

Using Qualifiers

"Not to be rude or offensive, but..."
"This could be a horrible idea, but..."
"I know what you're thinking, but..."

Qualifiers, i.e., little expressions said before or after a statement with the intention of softening or mitigating that statement, certainly have their place. Overusing them, though, can be pretty annoying. Why? In the right circumstances, they can come across as condescending and unneeded. Remember the manipulative communication style?

Nobody wants to feel like they are being managed or handled. If you go to great lengths to use qualifiers, it may stir up feelings of mistrust in your listener, who could wonder why you're not just being direct. Remind yourself that the world "but" is kind of magical—people tend to discount everything that came before that word! It's yet another barrier, albeit one that is mostly just annoying.

Equating Your Experiences

In Chapter 4, we'll look more closely at mastering the emotional aspects of effective communication, but for now, it's enough to banish this single meaningless phrase from your repertoire: "I know exactly how you feel!" It's even worse if you then proceed to tell a lengthy story about a time when you felt similarly despite the fact that the two situations are completely dissimilar.

Keep in mind that every person's journey is unique. It's good that you're making an effort to be empathetic. But think about it from the other side. Has hearing about someone else's hard time ever made *you* feel less unhappy about your own troubles? Probably not. Whether you can understand another person's experiences or not is irrelevant. Almost always it will not feel good for them to hear it.

Floundering

We've all encountered people who ramble on without a point as though they like the sound of their own voices. If you have a tendency to do this yourself, constantly try to remember how mind-numbing it is to be on the receiving end! Floundering and waffling on and on is usually a bad habit we get into when we're nervous or unconsciously afraid that something bad will happen unless we keep performing and filling the silence. But like every other poor communication strategy listed here, it doesn't work: The more we talk, the less people listen.

Think carefully, say what you need to say, and be straightforward and succinct when you talk. Have faith that you've been heard, and if you *haven't* been heard, just let it go, because it's likely that you would not have convinced anyone to care or understand simply by going on ad nauseum.

Waiting Instead of Listening

Everyone knows they should be a good listener. To be honest, most of us are better at acting the role of good listener than actually being one! Rather than listening with all our attention to what we're told, we are really just waiting our turn. Worse, we might be listening with an agenda—discarding what doesn't fit the agenda, hearing what we like, and spending the next few minutes drafting a witty response...just as soon as the other person stops talking. If this is a bad habit to break, remind yourself of the fact that people can usually *tell* when you're not listening. It's not easy to hide, and it makes you appear selfish, disinterested, and unkind.

Fluff and Filler Words.

Padding out your speech with filler words may be more or less acceptable depending on your age, culture, and social situation, but it's almost always better to avoid it entirely. Filler words are things like *um*, *ah*, *okay*, *like*, *you know*, *you see*, *uhh*, *right*, *kinda*, *so*, *actually*, *err*, *hmm*, and so on. You may in fact have your own personal verbal tic—for example, some people have a strange habit of ending every sentence with a dangling "so . . ." that doesn't go anywhere. Others will liberally sprinkle "like" or "um" everywhere. Still, others will have overused turns of phrase that add nothing at all to the message—for example, the woman who ends every simple phrase with, "if that makes sense?" or the guy who cannot open his mouth without saying, "yeah, well."

Try this challenge for yourself: Once you've identified your own pet filler words, try to consciously replace them with plain old silence. Just say nothing and pause until you can say something that isn't a filler word. If you can be mindful enough to do this in the moment, you may be surprised at just how polished and put together you come across. You don't have to say anything profound—just remove the filler words and you automatically seem more self-assured, authoritative, and sophisticated (note, of course, that if you deliberately don't want to appear that way, then ignore this advice!).

So interrupting, being distracted, trying to make every conversation about you . . . all these smaller conversation-killing habits are actually expressions of one deeper, bigger problem: conversational narcissism. We are all guilty of this to some extent. A conversation is about **two** people. Even beyond that, a good conversation is one where both people have actively participated, and both have **connected** with one another. That simply means that to the extent you are focusing only on *yourself*, the conversation will be lacking 41somehow. The more you can focus on the other person, the better the conversation will be. This realization seems pretty obvious on the face of it, yet look around and you will notice that almost all cases of miscommunication or failed connection come from, in one way or another, conversational narcissism. Whether the obstacles are psychological, behavioral, or just bad habits we've fallen into, if they put us at the center and cause us to forget the other person and their perspective, then our communication will never be everything it has the potential to be.

The Rapport Game

Imagine you are sitting across the street from a café and watching three tables, each with two people having a conversation. At Table A, both people are leaning in together, seemingly mimicking one another's facial expressions and hand gestures, while at Table B, the people talking are looking very serious and low energy, but they've both leaned back in their chairs and, just like Table A, seem to be mirroring one another's behavior. Table C is different—one person is seemingly excited and smiling, while the other is calmer, speaking less, and adopting a completely different posture and facial expression.

Without knowing anything about the content of the conversation, you can probably tell even from afar which conversations are going well and which one isn't!

That's because at its most fundamental, good **communication is NOT about the words you say but the degree of concordance, harmony, and synchronicity between you and the person you're talking to.**

So, this is exactly our next pitstop on our journey to becoming better communicators.

Mirroring and Matching

Have you ever actually wondered what "chemistry" is? That fizzle of energy and connection between two people is something that's difficult to describe, but you definitely know it when you feel it!

However mysterious it feels, this chemistry is actually well-explained as an evolutionary adaptation that has helped our species bond, connect, and establish trust . . . even *before* we developed verbal language. Mirroring and matching don't need much explanation—you've seen it with your own eyes! **When we match and mirror, we mimic not just what others say but how they say it, the words they use, their accents, turns of phrase, gestures, posture, voice tone, pitch and volume, and facial expressions.**

Here's the thing: We all instinctively know how to mirror and match; it's just that the more charismatic among us know how to do it *deliberately*.

In the 1970s, Richard Bandler and John Grinder introduced a communication theory they called Neuro-Linguistic Programming (NLP). They claimed that most people tend to feel happier and more comfortable around those who are similar to them—even if this recognition of similarity is largely unconscious.

Have you ever noticed two people get together for the first time and immediately start to look for things in common between them? They may smile as they both realize they grew up in the same area or liked the same shows when they were kids, or both indirectly know the same people. As they do this, they may start to reflect and mimic one another, matching the other's tone of voice, hand movements, and other idiosyncrasies. It's as though the more similar we feel to the person in front of us, the more we feel that they can hear and understand us, and the more we trust and like them.

> **Mirroring** is copying and reflecting a behavior in the same moment. So they smile, and you smile. They whisper, and so do you. Done right, it creates feelings of harmony and synchrony—like you're both doing a coordinated dance in time with one another.

> **Matching** is copying and reflecting, but not necessarily at the same time. So perhaps they use an unusual and noteworthy turn of phrase, which you remember and return to later in the conversation (almost literally communicating, "I speak the same language as you!").

The wonderful thing is that mirroring and matching can create strong feelings of harmony and connection even *without you saying a word*.

It's difficult to estimate just how much communication is nonverbal, but it's clear that the proportion is significant. Whether you're meeting someone new, talking to an old friend, or trying to navigate a prickly conflict, matching and mirroring is a great skill to master since it always gives you a solid base on which to build. There are three main ways to build rapport by using matching and mirroring.

Way 1: Match and Mirror External Communication Cues

Body language and nonverbal communication are prior to verbal communication. If you adopt the same posture as the person in front of you, you duplicate their experience in your own body and can understand more about their position—literally! You also communicate that you're on the same wavelength and will create feelings of being in sync.

In conversation, simply notice how **"open" or "closed" body language** as a whole seems. Look for tension (crossed arms, hunched posture, closed fists, frowning) or relaxation (open arms, expressive hands, legs uncrossed). Without aping them very obviously, try to match this degree of openness/closedness.

Next, notice **gestures**, i.e., body postures *in motion*. Are they moving quickly or slowly? Are they graceful and flowing or sharp and staccato?

Wide and expansive? Fidgety? Protective? Restrained? How do the gestures line up with everything else in the conversation? Match and mirror this.

You could also match and mirror **facial expressions**—in fact, you might find you do this automatically just by paying close attention to the other person! You could focus on just one most notable aspect—for example, the eyebrows or corners of the mouth. Again, see if you can match the position, movement, and degree of openness or closedness here, especially at points in the conversation when emotional content is being communicated. You could *say*, "I know how you feel," but when your facial expression matches theirs, you are doing something more powerful—you are *showing* that you understand what they mean.

Way 2: Match and Mirror Voice and Language

This is a rich area to tap! Consider all the aspects of the voice that have nothing to do with the words used:

- Tone
- Rate (speed)
- Volume (both loudness and simply the amount of speech)
- Pitch (how high or low)
- Pace, inflection, and modulation (how you deliver your sentences and the flow

of speech—for example, with lots of variation or with a steady, even monotone)

You can match and mirror on any of the above five aspects—or potentially all of them. The key, however, is to do this subtly and naturally. For example, if the person you're speaking to is talking quickly (fast rate), speaking quite loudly (high volume) and in a high pitch, and talking with an excitable and highly inflected tone, then you can signal your empathy and understanding of their frame of mind by mimicking some of this yourself. You could subtly raise your own pitch, talk a little louder than you ordinarily would, and mirror that excitement back at them. Overall, you are attempting to match the energy of what they're communicating. Just remember that the voice is a part of the body, and so every aspect of the voice is essentially body language.

One thing you might not have considered is what communication experts call sensory predicates. Basically, these are systems of meaning that we use to explain our experiences. We each have a system whether we're aware of it or not, i.e., we might favor descriptions and explanations that are

- Visual
- Auditory
- Kinesthetic

- Feeling

- Auditory Digital

A few examples will show how sensory predicates play out in real life. A visual predicate, for example, uses language, symbolism, and metaphors that are based in the physiology of sight. So, you might pepper your speech with terms like *picture this, look, view, bright, reveal, short-sighted, paint a picture, I can see, clear, dim*, etc.

Similarly, more auditory (to do with sound) predicates will include phrases like *listen, tell, clear as a bell, on the same frequency, lend me your ears, strike a note, loud and clear*, etc.

Kinesthetic and feeling predicates may overlap somewhat and mix both meanings of the word "feel"—for example, *I'm touched, concrete, solid, hot and bothered, get in touch, handhold, grasp, make contact*, etc.

So-called auditory digital predicates are more focused on the cognitive experience of the world—for example, with terms like *understand, know, think, process, figure it out, pay attention, wonder*, etc.

The point of understanding the predicates someone uses is so that you can match and mirror these, too. The result can be an instant connection and feeling of rapport. For example, if someone consistently uses visual predicates, they may say, "I like the look of this idea. You've painted such a clear picture of the most important goals." If you pick up on this, you can continue and expand the visual metaphors, or include your own by later saying something like, "I see what you mean! I'm glad we're focusing on the same vision here."

Now, this might not seem like much, but it's a powerful way to unconsciously signal that you speak the same language and, even more than this, inhabit the same perceptual world as the other person. If you're not entirely clear which kind of predicate the person is using, it's no big deal—simply prick your ears (there's an auditory one!) to the kinds of metaphors they use, and repeat or expand on them rather than abruptly switching to a different metaphor.

Way 3: Match and Mirror Internal Communication Cues

This one is a little less obvious. The voice and the body may be easier to notice at first glance, but have you ever simply felt that **people have different energy levels from each other**? This "energy" is about how active, energetic, and vibrant someone is, yes, but it can also be more subtle than this.

Think of someone who is really good at doing impressions. They are able to so perfectly capture another person's personality not just because they can mimic their voice and mannerisms, but also because somehow, they can put all these things together and portray the person's deeper essence. Noticing this essence takes practice, but at first, try to simply pay attention to how people are taking up space, how they're breathing, and the *aggregate* of all their expressions (language, posture, appearance) comes across.

Reflecting someone's essence may take a special touch, but you'd be surprised at how instantly you can create camaraderie if you can do so. If ever you're with someone and you just "click," try to see things from the other side and ask what the other person did to make you feel that communication and connection were so easy with them. Chances are it's mirroring!

Here's a little trick you can try not just to build rapport, but to test whether you are getting anywhere in that goal:

Step 1: Pay attention to their internal or external communication cues, or their voice or language.

Step 2: Match or mirror subtly on just one or two aspects.

Step 3: After a little while, match them on some other aspect.

Step 4: Finally, do something different. For example, if you've been mirroring a low and slow tone of voice, plus crossed legs, suddenly change up your voice and speak louder and more quickly, or uncross your legs and cross your arms instead.

Step 5: Now, observe. Do they follow suit and mirror *you*? If so, congratulations—you've likely established rapport! If not, no problem. There's still time.

As you get better at matching and mirroring (and conversation in general), you can start experimenting with *leading* interactions with certain behaviors rather than just following the other person's lead. This way, you can take charge of conversations and shape them in a positive direction, fostering connection and understanding—usually without the other person even knowing it!

Here's another trick you can try once you get the hang of reading other people's communication cues:

Step 1: Think of someone you have an excellent rapport with and try to feel what it feels like when you're around that person. Really recreate that experience in your body, heart, and mind.

Step 2: Consciously try to summon up that same feeling in yourself right now, imagining it expanding through your body. For example, maybe with a very good friend, you feel expansive, you're quick to smile, and you lean forward ever so slightly. Maybe you feel ultra-relaxed and "warm." Whatever the sensation is, imagine that it's surrounding you like an aura. Then, let it guide how you behave, think, feel, and move in the moment.

Step 3: Project the feeling toward the person you're with and imagine that this amazing aura is flowing around them, too.

This technique is taking a reverse perspective on mirroring, since you are the one who is "going first" and inviting others to mirror and match you—if you master those good, happy vibes, don't be surprised if people suddenly seem very willing to be drawn in!

Way 4: Match on Content

Basically, seek common ground. If people like people who are like them, then rapport is in some ways just a matter of finding how you're like the person in front of you.

Potential areas of common ground include:

- Your history and background, such as school, hometown, past jobs, shared connections
- Personal values, such as family, hard work, creativity, learning, etc.

- Core beliefs about the world
- Emotional state, both current and more generally in life
- Style
- Accent, ways of speaking, and verbal idiosyncrasies
- Hobbies
- Shared experiences
- Degree of formality (for example, do they use slang and swear words? Or are they very correct, polite, and articulate?), convention, class, age, or generation
- Personality differences (for example, some people bond over being flippant, quirky, serious-minded, poetic, spiritually inclined, straightlaced, mischievous, etc., but people can also differ in their focus on the bigger picture versus the details, the emotional versus the factual content of a conversation, or the overall volume of information they're comfortable exchanging)

Way 5: Chunking

One final way to establish effortless rapport is something you might not have considered before: carefully moderating the questions you ask people to control the level of detail of information you get. There are two different modes we can adopt any time we ask someone a question.

Chunking down is about diving down into details and going from the general to the specific. Questions that chunk down give more color, depth, and richness to the conversation; however, if you stay too long mired in the details, the conversation can quickly get lost, overwhelmed, or even boring. We ask a chunking-down question every time we want to learn more, and when we do so, we build rapport since we are showing interest in the real nitty-gritty of what we're told.

For example, we could ask,

"How exactly did that happen?"
"Tell me more about XYZ . . ."
"Why did this specific thing happen?"

Chunking up goes in the other direction, from the specific to the general. We ask a question that leads us to see the bigger picture and overarching patterns in the broader view—i.e., a model that fits all the smaller details inside it. When we ask questions in this mode, we are showing that we are paying attention and processing and synthesizing what we're told, which is a different way to build rapport.

For example, we could ask

"How does this tie into this other idea we spoke about, XYZ . . . ?"
"What do all of these details mean?"
"What's the pattern here?"
"What does this thing connect to?"

During conversations, it's not really a matter of which question mode is "best" but rather keeping things varied. Imagine you are zooming in and out, first drilling down to learn more about the most interesting details, then coming up for air and getting a broader view. Not only will such a conversation feel like it flows more naturally and enjoyably, your dynamic interest in what you're being told will create a sense of rapport with the other person.

At the very least, simply avoid being in one mode for too long. So, for example, if you notice that you've asked five chunking-up questions in a row, be aware that you may be alienating the other person in overly abstract or aloof hypotheticals. Create balance by asking a detailed question, which will bring in some immediacy and intimacy.

Similarly, if you notice the conversation is feeling a little mired in one detail after another (for example, those conversations where people lose a narrative thread because they dwell too long on the minute but insignificant details of who said what and when . . .) then pause, zoom out, and get a broader view of where you are. You might say something like, "So all in all, it seems like yesterday was a pretty crazy day, huh!"

Expressing Without Speaking

How do you "read" people's nonverbal communication?

Words are not the only things that carry meaning. Appearance, objects, sound, fragrance, and even space all have socially shared significance. **Communication, therefore, includes expressions of the entire body, movement, gesture, physical orientation, and a range of "paralinguistic" cues already discussed, such as voice pitch, volume, and intonation**. Proximity, color, even time—almost anything can serve as a carrier of meaning and therefore be used in human communication.

How to Read Microexpressions

A microexpression is a quick (just 0.5 to 4 seconds) and involuntary facial expression produced when experiencing an emotion. Microexpressions are genuine, meaning they cannot be faked or concealed, and this makes them an ideal behavior to observe when with other people. The reasoning is that if you can accurately understand the emotional state of the person in front of you, communication automatically becomes easier, more direct, and more real.

It's possible that you are already able to read microexpressions, but do so unconsciously. Have you ever spoken to someone and, even though they said all the right things and appeared to be smiling, you still got a gut feeling that they were upset? You might have come to this conclusion because your unconscious mind noticed the genuine microexpression of anger and knew that this revealed the true feeling. What we might do unconsciously can be done with more deliberation and practice.

Basically, the seven primary human emotions come from universal physiological responses to the environment. Microexpressions are quicker, more subtle versions of the more obvious "macroexpressions" you're already familiar with. As you read the following descriptions, try to mirror and match them, and see how quickly you start to feel the emotion they represent!

Surprise

- Raised and curved eyebrows.
- Stretched skin below the brow.
- Horizontal wrinkles across the forehead.
- Eyelids open, with the white of the eye showing all around the iris.
- Jaw open and teeth parted, but without tension in the mouth.

Fear

- Eyebrows raised and knotted together.
- Forehead wrinkled in the center and not straight across.
- Upper eyelid raised, with lower lid also tense and drawn up.
- Eyes show white above the iris, but not below it.
- Mouth open, with lips slightly tense or stretched back.

Disgust

- Eyes narrowed.
- Upper lip lifted.
- Upper teeth potentially exposed.
- Nose wrinkled.
- Cheeks raised.

Anger

- Eyebrows lowered and pulled together.

- Vertical lines between the eyebrows.
- Lower lip tightened.
- Eyes staring or bulging.
- Lips can be pursed, corners down, or in a square shape, as if shouting.
- Nostrils may be widened.
- Lower jaw juts forward.

Happiness

- Corners of the lips pulled back and up.
- Mouth may or may not be parted, teeth shown.
- A wrinkle appears from outer nose to outer lip.
- Cheeks raised.
- Lower eyelid may wrinkle or tighten a little.
- Crow's feet appear at the corners of the eyes.

Sadness

- Inner corners of eyebrows drawn in and up.
- Corner of the lips drawn down.
- Jaw comes up.
- Lower lip pouts.

Contempt / Hate

- Fairly neutral expression.

- One side of the mouth raised.

Noticing microexpressions is only the beginning. What do you do with your observations? There are two possibilities:

1. The microexpression **aligns with** what is being said, in which case there is additional information and body language to add dimension to what is being communicated to you.

2. Or, the microexpression in fact **contradicts** what is being said. In this case, you can assume that the person is concealing something (or flat out deceiving you or themselves), or else they are conflicted and wearing a kind of mask. But again, this simply adds more data to your reading of them.

Posture and Body Orientation

People's postures can reveal a great deal about them. Have you ever failed to comprehend what the other person was truly thinking when you were texting them and, as a result, had an awkward misunderstanding? This probably happened because an important channel of information was closed off to you both—the nonverbal body-language cues that would have allowed you to fine-tune your conversation.

Let's revisit the idea of "open" and "closed" body posture. Rather than taking any single action in isolation ("crossed arms means you're angry, a toe pointing toward the door means you want to run away," and so on . . .), observe the entire body as one unit.

An open posture portrays friendliness, receptivity, and positivity.

The feet are spread wide, and the palms of your hands are exposed and facing outward/visible.

It's easy to see if someone's overall demeanor is communicating openness, but it's just as important to be self-aware and make sure that you are also communicating the right message with open postural language. Keep a straight spine with your head lifted, open the chest and relax the shoulders down, loosen your facial features, and turn your entire body to face the other person.

A closed posture portrays boredom, hostility, or detachment.

The impression is one of tension and tightness. Arms and legs may be crossed; the features of the face will be tight, clenched, or pulled; hands will be closed or grasping; and the body will either seem to be hunched or crumpled in on itself, or else stiff and immobile, perhaps with shoulders held too high.

Many so-called body language experts will go into great detail about what this or that tiny movement or gesture means, but this is usually unnecessary. You can achieve an incredible amount of insight into the person in front of you by simply asking whether they are open or closed, and further whether their posture aligns with their verbal expression or contradicts it.

Reading body language is not a foolproof science, but rather a way to collect observations and seek out patterns. There are two rules to effective body language reading:

1. No single detail is decisive and conclusive
2. Consider every observation against a baseline

For example, if you notice that someone's arms are crossed, you'd be wrong to conclude solely based on this observation that they are angry or closed off. Perhaps it's winter and they're simply cold. This is why you need to consider context and a *range* of observations, seeking repeated patterns rather than just a single isolated behavior. If they're scowling, crossing their arms, *and* turning away from you, the conclusion that they're angry holds more weight.

Imagine that you one day receive a warm hug and a big smile from someone you've just met. Are they coming on to you? Don't assume they are until you know what their baseline is, i.e., what is "normal" for them. Notice that they hug and smile at everyone all the time, and your observations suddenly don't imply flirtatiousness anymore!

Eye Contact

The eyes are such an important and expressive part of the human body that they get classed as a form of communication all their own, not to mention assumed to be the windows to the soul and one of the focal points (there's a visual predicate right there!) of love poetry the world over.

First things first: eye contact in itself is neither good nor bad. Rather, it's a question of *how* you make it, when, and why. More is not always better. When you're making eye contact with someone you've just met and don't know very well, the mere act of lingering your gaze on theirs for slightly longer than is comfortable is a courageous way to signal that you are wanting to up the intensity and get to know the person a little better. If they match and mirror this eye contact, consider that your message has been heard and the response is broadly positive.

Better eye contact skills will reap benefits in the workplace, will make you a better public speaker, will help you smooth over conflicts, and will make you appear more charismatic to the opposite sex.
In a study led by Dr. Arthur Aron, men and women were put into opposite sex pairs and asked to look into each other's eyes for two minutes straight. These couples later reported feelings of attraction, affection, and even love for the people they originally met as strangers. Surprisingly, one of the couples even married! So, the eyes are powerful communicators.

Eye contact can create intimacy and intensity, but too much can be disastrous. Whatever you do, you don't want your eye contact to be **inappropriate** or **unwelcome**. Don't stare at people. If you're looking at them and they look away to avoid your gaze and then return their gaze, and you are still looking at them, this will feel intrusive and even violating to them.

In his book, *The Power of Eye Contact*, psychologist Michael Ellsberg explains,

> "In order for eye contact to feel good, one person cannot impose his visual will on another; it is a shared experience.

Perhaps eyes meet only for a second at first; one partner then tests the waters and tries a few seconds, and when that is met warmly, the pair can begin ramping up the eye contact together until they are locked in a beautiful dance of eyes and gazes."

A good rule of thumb is to be brave and initiate eye contact, but after two unsuccessful attempts to catch their eye, stop. Be mindful of the rest of your body language, and moderate yourself. Eye contact plus leaning back may make the intimacy a little more comfortable, whereas eye contact *and* close proximity *and* intense language can be overwhelming.

Another good idea is to take frequent pauses—a little eye contact goes a long way. Rest your gaze elsewhere for a while (look to the side, not down), or try career expert Kara Ronin's "triangle technique" to cut potential awkwardness:

1. Draw an imaginary inverted triangle on the other person's face around their eyes and mouth.
2. During the conversation, change your gaze every five to ten seconds from one point on the triangle to another. This will make you look interested and engrossed in the conversation without coming across as creepy!

Paralinguistics

As you become a more active speaker and listener, increasing your awareness of the subtle nuances of verbal communication can contribute significantly to the quality of the conversation you have with others. This awareness will also promote a deeper understanding of, and connection with, those around you.

When you speak, you expose a great deal about yourself, much of which frequently has nothing at all to do with the words you are using. The term "paralinguistics" refers to the study of voice **tone, volume, inflection, and pitch** and other components of nonverbal vocal communication that we've already briefly explored.

Pay attention to your own voice and its function—it takes effort and practice to become a comfortable, conscious speaker. Think about how much of an impact your vocal inflection can have on the interpretation of what you're saying. It's possible to communicate either extreme happiness or else anger and contempt—while using the very same words!

How people deliver their words is as important as the words themselves. Become aware both of what you are communicating as well as what others are communicating with you, and your powers of communication will strengthen enormously.

The Four Ps of Voice

Imagine that speaking is like a train ride—peaks and valleys are more exciting and adventurous, while flat, unchanging terrain is not. Try to vary your speed and speak so as to include peaks, valleys, flat terrains, and pauses. Likewise, listen to the "landscape" of other people's speech and see what it tells you about their state of mind and the message they're sharing beyond the words they use.

1. **Power/Projection:** how loud or soft you speak

Modify your voice projection and speak loudly if you're addressing more people. A confident speaker has good projection. Low projections make listeners lean forward to listen. When telling a secret (or wanting people to come closer to you), employ low projection.

2. **Pace:** how fast or slowly you speak

Quick speech implies nervousness, energy, enthusiasm, force, or even fear. Slow speech can convey calmness and gravity—or else be boring.

Be animated and vary the speed of your speech depending on the effect you want it to have on others.

3. **Pitch:** high or low

Pitch conveys emotion—high pitch reflects wrath, happiness, surprise, or excitement. Low pitch expresses power, relaxation, aggression, or sadness.

4. **Pause:** quiet moments bring emphasis or allow listeners to absorb and process

Poor communicators think that a pause is asking to be interrupted or an admission that you forgot what you were saying. But skilled conversationalists know that pauses are powerful; they use them to add significance to their words and pace themselves, keeping their listeners on board with what they're saying. Advanced speakers use a pause to optimize their speech's impact on their audience.

How to Improve Your Vocal Variety

So, how do you know whether to pause or not? How do you know when to talk more quickly or loudly or with a higher pitch? Well, imagine that all the shades and nuances available in your voice are like colors in a palette. Whatever you're communicating, you can paint a more powerful picture for the other person if you're using a full, rich palette of colors.

"Vocal variety" is a little like being physically flexible and fit—it means we are familiar with and comfortable using the full range of our voice's potential. And like physical fitness, we can train this variety. Here are a few ideas.

- Before you socialize, literally warm up your vocal cords, like an actor before a rehearsal. Massage your cheeks and jaw and practice saying *mamamama* and *wawawawa* sounds, or do "lip trills" where you forcefully blow "raspberries" by expelling a stream of air through pursed lips. This develops both breath and vocal control.
- Practice diaphragm breathing. Place one hand on your belly and one on your chest and take deep breaths so that only your belly hand rises. After a few breaths, see if you can speak a long, slow sentence on one full belly breath. Play around with what it feels like to control this stream of air so that your voice is calm and measured.
- Pick a random passage of text (children's storybooks are great for this) and read through the passage, first in a dull monotone. Then, read through it again,

trying to add as much color as possible—change your pitch, pacing, tone—be dramatic! Interactions can be awkward at first simply because you're using vocal muscles that are not warmed up. Warm up this way and you'll feel more vocally limber when you next enter a conversation.
- If you find that your pitch gets uncomfortably high or low, or that you are often breathless or struggle to moderate volume, consider taking up singing to help improve your vocal mastery. Even chanting can help!
- An alternative is to take up improv classes or learn to do a little acting. When you think of your voice as an expressive and artistic tool, you become far more aware of its power—and how you can use this power according to your own ends.

The irony is that the better you are able to master and control your own voice, and the more self-awareness you have around your voice, the better you will become at hearing other people's voices in three dimensions! You will notice the breathless or choked quality in a friend's speech and understand that they're nervous. You'll notice the subtle change in pitch that signals someone's rising excitement . . . and know exactly how to match them to show your synchrony and support for that excitement. Communication is not just vocal, but that doesn't mean that the voice isn't an extremely powerful and flexible tool that lets you communicate anything and everything.

Summary:

- The best mindset to adopt in order to become a better communicator is the one that will best allow you to connect, meet your needs, solve problems, and express yourself.
- Begin by asking yourself what your default communication style is: aggressive, passive-aggressive, or manipulative. None of these styles actually achieves the ultimate goal of communication, however.
- The way you communicate is a choice. Assertive communication is the ability to express needs, wants, thoughts, and feelings directly without disrespecting or controlling others. Mature conversationalists are self-controlled, balanced, relaxed, open, and respectful.
- Communicating well is simple and easy, but we need to remove the formidable psychological barriers that stand in the way. With awareness, we can remove them and improve our communication skills.
- Barriers to good conversation include assumptions, strong negative emotions like

anger and aggression (which inspire defensiveness), preconceived ideas and prejudice, fear, inflexibility and a need to control, premature evaluation and judgment, and other negative conversational habits like interrupting or one-upping.
- Good conversation is firstly about the degree of concordance, harmony, and synchronicity between you and the person you're talking to, i.e., rapport.
- We can increase rapport by mirroring and matching both nonverbal and verbal expression. This can be done with internal and external cues, voice and language, content, and chunking style (i.e., up or down).
- When reading someone's body language, pay attention to microexpressions, their overall posture and orientation in space, as well as their degree of eye contact. Paralinguistics refers to information carried in the tone, pace, pitch, etc. of the voice.
- Think in terms of overall openness or closedness, but remember that no single detail is decisive and conclusive, and that observations should always be compared against a baseline.

Chapter 2. Tools of the Charming

Have Better Conversations with the Rule of Three

The rules for good communication are pretty basic.

Talk WITH people and not TO them.

Be present.

Listen.

Easy, huh?

Yet somehow, almost all of us could stand to be better conversationalists. The irony is that nobody ever wakes up in the morning and says to themselves, "Today, I'm going to be a complete bore to talk to." Nobody wants to be that person who constantly one-ups everyone else, interrupts, or talks too much.

Here's a rule for good communication that you might not have considered: **Having charm and**

charisma is not about you. It's about the other person.

So many of us embark on a mission to be more interesting and likeable in conversation, but just by having this attitude, we sabotage ourselves. Why? Because we have it backward. Being a great communicator is not about having other people listen to you, like you, or compliment you. It's about you making other people feel heard, liked, and praised.

The irony is that when we try too hard to be witty and impressive, our focus narrows down to our own egos, and we instantly become the opposite of what we're hoping to be. The other person disappears, and we are engaging in what is, for all intents and purposes, a boring monologue.

Lecture, consultant, author, and coach Dr. Karl Albrecht explained in *Psychology Today* that every conversation is made up of three key elements:

1. Declaratives
2. Questions
3. Qualifiers

Declaratives are simply statements of fact—for example, "The sky is light blue."

However, to make things more complicated, they aren't always exactly facts, but opinions that are presented *as though* they are facts:

"Light blue is too weak a color to wear to that job interview."

Questions are self-explanatory (although this doesn't include rhetorical questions that take the grammatical form of a question but are not literally asking the other person to respond—for example, "What is it with this weather today?").

What's your favorite color?

What should I wear to the interview?

Finally, **qualifiers** are something we've encountered already and include any words or phrases intended to soften or moderate what is being said. For example:

"In my opinion . . ."

"I'm wondering if . . ."

"I could be wrong, but as far as I know . . ."

"I'm not speaking for everyone here, but . . ."

Qualifiers are also great at helping you express uncertainty or make a claim—but not too strongly. So instead of saying that light blue *is* a weak color, you could say it *might be* a *slightly* weak color. Instead of saying, "Freud was a pervert," you say, "In my opinion, it may be the case that Freud in fact had a distorted sexuality."

Now, Albrecht suggested what he calls the "rule of three." Simply, in a conversation, **make sure**

that you are never making three declarative statements in a row. Instead, include plenty of questions or qualifiers (i.e., softer and more moderate declaratives) to give your speech a little more flexibility. Crucially, doing so will make sure that the conversation doesn't become bogged down in ego and narcissism.

A question is a way to bat the conversational ball over the net and to the other person, who is then invited to say what they want to before batting the ball back again. A modifier is halfway between a question and a declarative statement—you say what you want to say, but you leave a little room in there for someone else to add what they want to. There is nothing wrong with a declarative per se—but it is the sort of thing that closes off any avenues for connection (beyond bland agreement or outright disagreement, that is—both of which do not actually further the conversation).

Try it, and you may be surprised at just how much more your conversations flow—and you'll come across as more likeable, too. Understanding the rule of three means you won't soon run out of things to say in any conversation. You can basically never go wrong if you a) ask a question or b) say whatever declarative statement you were just about to say but soften it a qualifier.

Consider the following conversation:

Person A: I've got this really bad shoulder pain . . . the physiotherapist says it's bursitis!

Person B: Wow, bursitis? My grandmother had that last year. It's more common than you think, you know.

Person A: Yeah, well, it's the first I've heard of it. Apparently, it was most likely caused by the Covid vaccine.

Person B: Well, you have to consider all the possible causes—there are lots of things that could be to blame. It's actually repetitive strain that causes most cases of bursitis.

Person A: Sure, yeah. Anyway, my physiotherapist said it's an injury that can happen when the needle is placed just slightly in the wrong place . . .

Person B: A lot of those people giving vaccines didn't get the right training.

Person A: Well, let me tell you, it hurts like hell!

Person B: I'm sure. The best thing would be to have plenty of rest, I guess.

Now take a look at the above conversation and ask yourself how much you like Person B. They are not being a conversational narcissist in the sense that it's all me, me, me . . . but somehow, their ego seems to loom large in the above exchange. Why? You'll notice that everything that Person B says is a declarative statement. It gives the conversation a flat, dead feeling. After a declarative, there's not much to do except agree, disagree, or stop talking. In the extreme, too many declaratives like this can actually make the person seem as though they are lecturing, preaching, or explaining . . . i.e., it can feel very dull and even condescending!

Let's look at a different conversation:

Person A: I've got this really bad shoulder pain . . . the physiotherapist says it's bursitis!

Person C: Wow, bursitis? My grandmother had that last year. It's more common than you think, you know.

Person A: Yeah, well, it's the first I've heard of it. Apparently, it was most likely caused by the Covid vaccine.

Person C: Really? That's interesting. Do you mean you had a bad reaction to something that was in the vaccine?

Person A: Actually, no. My physiotherapist said it's an injury that can happen when the needle is placed just slightly in the wrong place.

Person C: Ouch! Well, I may be wrong about this, but I seem to remember reading an article last year about how many volunteers had emergency training to learn to give the vaccine. Maybe the person who jabbed you just wasn't all that experienced?

Person A: Yeah, exactly, that's what I think too. It's annoying because it really hurts!

Person C: I can imagine. What do you think you'll do now? Have you got something relaxing planned for the weekend?

First, just ask yourself which person—Person B or Person C—you feel is more likable. The two conversations are very, very similar. Both are perfectly acceptable, and there is no offense caused or any major rupture in social etiquette in either one. And yet, even in this short interaction, you can probably see the big difference the rule of three makes and how a person using declaratives one hundred percent comes across so differently from someone using a mix of all three conversational types.

Person B likely doesn't believe themselves to be bad at conversation, but they nevertheless will be perceived as less friendly, less likeable, and somehow less enjoyable to speak to. The effect of such interactions gradually and imperceptibly adds up. Others may not be able to put their finger on why, but they may feel that Person B is a bit boring, stuck-up, rude, or a know-it-all.

Crucially, it's not about the content of what you say. It's about the emotional implications and the energy in *how* you say it.

Questions convey a sense of openness, possibility, humility, and receptivity. They can be playful and respectful and can demonstrate empathy and compassion, as well as the covert message, "I like you. I'm interested. Tell me more."

Qualified statements send a similar message. They say something, but it's a soft something. They signal to the other person that you are amenable, flexible, and ready to discuss and move with the flow.

Declaratives, however, are a little like dead-ends. They are pronouncements made that usually signal the *end* of conversation rather than its beginning. They position you as a speaker with authority, and the other person as someone who is there primarily to hear this authority. Though there is absolutely a time and place for this energy (giving speeches, setting boundaries, or literally teaching someone) too much of it means you are talking AT rather than talking WITH.

In other words, questions and qualifiers open up a little room that invites the other person into the conversation. Declaratives tend to focus only on you and your message, while closing out the other person.

"Light blue is such a weak color." Is it? Says who? Literally imagine someone said this to you—can you feel how difficult it is to say anything in response?

"Maybe it's an unpopular opinion, but I've never really liked light blue!" Can you see how it's possible to have a strong opinion but nevertheless frame it as exactly that—an opinion—and leave plenty of space for someone to respond and keep the conversation going?

"What's your favorite color?" A question immediately opens up the conversation and signals that you are willing and able to share airtime, to listen, and to connect. It's a signal that you are putting your ego aside and making space for connection, and even though it's subtle, it conveys feelings of appreciation and generosity that are worth their weight in gold.

By the way, it's worth noting that you don't have to become passive and unopinionated to be more likable. In fact, occasionally saying something *obviously* outrageous is a great way to inject a little playfulness into a conversation and get things flowing. But note that these declaratives are in a way acting like questions or qualifiers, since they can't help but draw the other person in.

"Oh, I simply cannot wear light blue. It makes my eyeballs itchy just looking at it."

"Man, I hate light blue. They should make convicts wear it in prison as punishment."

If the rule of three feels tricky to implement at first, don't worry—it can take time to break bad habits! One easy trick is to literally say whatever you were going to, but add "don't you think?" to the end of it. "Light blue is such a weak color, don't you think?" It immediately changes the entire energy and flow of the conversation and takes little-to-no effort on your part. Another trick to try is to simply convert any statement into a slightly softened question. Instead of saying "The blue looks weird," say "Do you think the blue looks a little off?"

If you're the kind of person who likes to get on a soapbox and bombard people with your strongly held opinions, try to ask yourself *why*. Being dogmatic and lecturing people and forcefully pushing your opinions on them is not communication, but a roadblock to communication. People can veer toward declarative statements that are opinions dressed up as facts for a few reasons:

- We unconsciously think that the purpose of a conversation is to have our needs met and to be heard and seen by someone else
- We may hold a core belief that we have to broadcast, defend, or force our perspectives and opinions, usually because they have not been appreciated or respected in the past

- We are anxious and trying to win validation or appear smart and interesting

The irony is that using the rule of three is something you do for other people—but it's ultimately something that benefits you. Conversations that are more balanced just flow better and lead to more comfort, trust, enjoyment, and attraction than ones where one or both parties are talking forcefully at the other, who is simply trying to endure it—or waiting for their own turn on the soapbox!

You'll notice as well that this trick works seamlessly with all the other advice we've covered so far. The rule of three helps you build rapport, removes barriers to connection, and helps you maintain a communication style that is relaxed and appealing.

Sustain Conversations with Conversational Threading and Useful Acronyms

Using the rule of three is all very well and good, but many people may find that this isn't quite enough. In casual conversation with new acquaintances, it can be really awkward: How do you know what to say? After the initial greetings and "how are yous" are done, then what?

Some people are masters at starting conversations, but this energy fizzles out quickly and they find that they cannot deepen the connection to the next level. Perhaps you know somebody who is like this: They are perfectly friendly and amiable, you like them and enjoy their company ... but somehow you never quite get past small talk and into anything juicier.

There can be a few reasons for this, but the solution is easy. Think of a relationship with someone as a piece of fabric. In the beginning, you literally just have a single thread with them. Your job is to spin that thread up and keep it strong, preventing it from snapping or getting knotted. If you talk to them again, you get the opportunity to create another thread. However, the "fabric" of your connection with them will be stronger if you can actively link up this new thread with the old one—weave them together. Otherwise, you risk spinning up that same thread over and over again from scratch, and you never weave a larger, two-dimensional piece of fabric at all.

Relationships take time. They are built out of all these conversational threads, thin as each one is on its own. The more there are, and the more connected they are, the more you will feel that your sense of rapport with the other person is deepening. Human beings are actually quite simple in this regard: they learn to trust and like what is repeated, predictable, and pleasant. Plus, they make meaning from *connections*—unless your interaction with them connects to something, it will be quickly forgotten.

It starts in the early stages with just keeping that thread spinning. **Using the technique of conversational threading, you will never run out of things to say.** The idea is simple:

1. The other person speaks, and you listen
2. You notice a few "threads" that they start
3. As the conversation unfolds, you pick up a thread and talk about it
4. When you run out of things to say, you *go back* and find an old thread and follow that instead
5. *Voila*, your conversation is running smoothly and comfortably!

Let's take a closer look. A "thread" is what it sounds like—a word, phrase, image, or idea that is shared by the other person. It can be literally anything. For example, if the other person says, "Since both of my brother's kids got diagnosed with ADHD, we're all trying to cut down on screen time." There are quite a few threads in this statement—at least four. There's the brother, the brother's kids, the fact of having less screen time, and the idea about ADHD diagnoses.

As you listen, hear these threads and pick them up. For example:

- "Oh, is that your brother you said lived abroad?"
- "How old are your brother's kids?"
- "Yup, I can relate. I've been trying to manage my own internet addiction these days!"
- "Wow, ADHD in *both* kids . . . I wonder how common that is."

As you can see, you can pick up a thread and ask a question about it, or just react and make a comment. But as you can imagine, each of these threads leads somewhere else. One will result in a long and impassioned conversation about the perils of TV on developing brains, while some others might fizzle out after a few short responses. For example, "Yeah, he's my older brother. He's currently living in Belgium with his family."

Should you happen to talk a little more about Belgium or living abroad and find that eventually that avenue runs dry, you don't need to worry. You can backtrack, drop the brother/Belgium thread, and pick up somewhere else. Of course, to do this effectively, you need to really pay attention and remember what you're told! Store those little threads for later.

"So anyway, was their ADHD diagnosis done there in Belgium?"

Two things have happened now. You have communicated to the other person that you were listening and paying attention, but you've also gently pivoted away from a dying topic and into one that might be more fruitful and interesting. Rather than it feeling like you're flitting from one shallow talking point to the next, though, it will seem as though the conversation is naturally developing and deepening.

One way to make sure this is happening is with (surprise surprise!) questions—but questions that probe a little deeper each time. So your first question might be about the plain facts and details of who lives where and how old they are. The next time you pick up this thread, though, you can ask about how people *felt* about these details. What do they want to do next? Why? What does all this suggest about their values, their sense of meaning and purpose? Note that you can do all this without it feeling like you're grilling them or hunting out juicy gossip. Start by sharing a little something of yourself to set the tone—for example, "You know, looking back I have wondered if I maybe had ADHD as a kid. On the other hand, I'm not sure whether being diagnosed back then would have changed who I am today, you know?"

The thread continues, but it's deepening and gathering meaning as it goes. You could do this with every one of the four threads above, even returning to certain ideas days or weeks later. You're weaving that fabric. Without them even realizing it, the other person may start to find you trustworthy and relatable, all while feeling that they are talking about *themselves*!

In real life, skilled conversationalists tend to practice conversation threading without even knowing it. But if you're the sort of person who gets anxious about being on the spot with nothing to say, conversation threading may be just the thing to come to your rescue. Here are a few ideas to make it even more effective:

- As you listen, prick your ears for words that suggest a **strong emotional component** for the speaker. Pull out particularly vivid images or unusual turns of phrase, or notice when the speaker gets a little more animated, and zoom in on that topic. It's likely going to be the most interesting thread to pursue! (Note: it's a bad idea, however, to pull on a thread where the emotion is obvious avoidance and discomfort—it's a quick way to be perceived as nosy or a bully.)
- When asking questions, keep them as **open-ended** as possible. "So, you have a brother?" might literally be something to fill the silence, but it can only be answered with "yup," which then promptly leaves you just where you started. Don't put the other person in the

position of having to think of things to say.
- As you listen for threads, don't be in too much of a hurry to pounce on them or forcefully steer the conversation. Just relax, **be patient**, and hold on to them. Even better if you can remember them for long after the current conversation is over. You will come across as attentive and aware and will win major conversational brownie points! "Hey, I had a new client from Belgium yesterday, and he reminded me about your brother. How's he doing, by the way?"

People who find conversations difficult are usually no less interesting, intelligent or kind than people find this kind of socializing easier. The only difference is that they are unaware of the practical skills required to have a great conversation . . . or else they know what to do but are out of practice!

At first, using the techniques and tricks outlined in this book will feel a little awkward and uncomfortable, but over time and with practice, you will internalize a deeper mindset shift and these behaviors will start to be second nature to you. Keep relaxed, keep listening, and keep the focus on the other person and you can't go too far wrong.

The bigger mindset shift that will come about by using conversational threading is one of

non-resistance. This means that when people introduce a thread, you listen, you're open and receptive, and you remember. You never forcefully cling to one thread over another, but stay relaxed and spontaneous in the moment, waiting to see what interesting things bubble up, and following them.

This is the kind of thing you need to *experience* rather than read about, though, so it's best to try these techniques for yourself. In particular, notice when you have a fixed idea of what you want to say or where you want the conversation to go. Notice if you're being resistant or forceful when it looks like the conversation is going elsewhere—then choose to let it go. If you quietly rehearse things in your head or keep forcefully bringing the conversation back to the point you want to make, the conversation will sputter out or die.

This is why we need to be brave enough to enter into conversations *without* being too prepared—if we have too fixed an idea of how things should go, we are not really listening for opportunities for it to be something better!

Useful Conversational Acronyms

The acronym HPM can be of great help when you feel yourself floundering for something to say, especially if you're talking to someone who's a little dull or not doing much to keep the conversation going. It stands for:

History

Philosophy

Metaphor

Don't worry, history doesn't literally refer to your knowledge of WWII and so on, but is about your own personal history and experience. You mention something in your own past that connects to what has just been said. Let's say someone mentions skydiving. You could say,

"That reminds me of a friend I had who went skydiving once. She was so terrified, she changed her mind right at the last moment and then..."

"Sounds like that one time I fell out of a second-story window... I know it's not skydiving, but it sure did feel like it at the time!"

"I knew a skydiving instructor once. Crazy guy."

Philosophy is about your own personal take on certain experiences, i.e., how you feel about things.

"Oh my God. You could not pay me enough money to consider sky diving! How terrifying!"

"One day, maybe for my fortieth birthday, I'll do skydiving. Wouldn't that be amazing?"

"So because he's a teacher, he sometimes does jumps *every day*—like, I said, crazy!"

Finally, metaphor is simply where you draw connections and make associations between what you know and what you've just heard.

"You know, that makes me think of this thing I saw on TV last night; these guys do what they call *extreme ironing*. Have you heard of this?"

"Wow, sky diving! That's like paying someone to pretend you're committing suicide, right?"

"That reminds me, I should renew my life insurance."

If you like, you can find a way to combine all three of these at one go:

Person A: "You'll never guess what. I'm going skydiving this weekend."

Person B: "Oh, wow, good for you!"

Person A: "I'm pretty terrified, but I'm trying new things, you know? Have you done it?"

Person B: "Oh, totally. I mean, there was that time I fell out of a second-story window . . . I know it's not exactly skydiving, but it sure did feel like it at the time! That reminds me, I should renew my life insurance."

Naturally, use HPM in the beginning of conversations or when you're trying to jump-start a flagging dialogue. It's a bad idea to jump in with your own jokes, anecdotes, or random connections if the conversation is actually already flowing well and the other person still wants to follow the current thread. Use HPM instead when things feel like they need a boost.

Another useful acronym is EDR:

Emotion

Detail

Restatement

Emotion is when you put a label on what someone else is feeling—for example, someone tells you a lengthy story about a recent trip to the ER, and you respond with, "Wow, it seems like it was a pretty scary time for you." You'll recognize that this is more or less the same skill as labeling or mirroring the other person's emotions.

Detail is asking for more in-depth information about what you've just been told, not unlike the "chunking down" discussed earlier. It could also mean answering a question but adding an additional detail to keep the conversation going. Detail questions are actually pretty easy to ask—just remember the 5 Ws: who, what, where, when, and why. For example, "So how long were you in the ER for? Hopefully they didn't keep you overnight."

Restatement is simple reflection and verbal mirroring. Repeat what you've been told, and you achieve three things at once: You show that you're listening attentively, you confirm that you understand and comprehend, and you validate the other person. Obviously don't literally parrot a person word for word, but choose a few key phrases or words to echo.

Person A: "I broke my arms doing extreme ironing, you see."

Person B: "Extreme ironing!"

Person A: "Yeah. I know it sounds funny, but I'm bummed out because I won't be able to make the championships this year."

Person B: "The championships?"

Person A: "Yup. I was totally in the running for a gold medal, but now who knows."

Person B: "Huh. A gold medal in extreme ironing."

A little hint: the more excited someone is, and the more they want to talk, the easier it will be to show your support simply by restatement. If the other person is reserved or unexcited, there might not be much to restate, or the conversation will stall without you injecting a little more into it.

In later chapters, we'll be looking at more in-depth techniques for communicating with empathy and cultivating deep listening. But with everyday conversations, it's all about **staying open, staying loose, and staying curious.** Think of the energy of a good conversation as a balloon that you have to constantly bounce to keep from touching the floor. Pleasant conversation has a lightness, movement, and spontaneity to it—you've probably experienced this yourself when having a really good time with someone.

If you're ever stuck and find yourself feeling unconfident in a conversation, try these three simple things to get you back on track:

1. Take a deep, deep breath and relax every muscle in your body
2. Ask a genuine, interesting open-ended question that puts the other person in the spotlight
3. Smile!

Summary:

- Having charm and charisma is not about you. It's about the other person and making them feel heard, liked, and supported.
- Dr. Albrecht explains that conversations contain three elements: declaratives, questions, and qualifiers. The rule of three tells us that we should not have three declarative statements in a row and should

- instead mix it up with a question or a qualifier.
- It's not really about the content of what you say but the emotional implications and the energy in *how* you say it.
- Conversational threading is a technique that will help you ensure you never run out of things to say. Listen to what the other person says, pick out a few noteworthy threads, then run with one of them. When the conversation dries up, return to these threads and pick up another one and follow that instead. Be patient, ask open-ended questions, and listen for emotions.
- Being a good everyday conversationalist is about being open-minded, spontaneous, and genuine. Keep things flowing!

Chapter 3. EQ > IQ

When you are able to suspend your own assumptions and biases, when you can adopt an attitude of openness and curiosity, and when you can let go of judgment, all your negative conversational habits will start to drift away . . . and in their place, something else will appear: *a growing awareness of the other person.*

As we become better communicators, we develop awareness of our own limitations, needs, desires, and idiosyncrasies. The interesting thing is, the better we can do this, the more aware we are of other people and everything they bring to the table. In other words, we develop emotional intelligence.

The concept of emotional intelligence was first introduced in the '90s by Peter Salovey and John D. Mayer. Later, the term was popularized by Daniel Goleman, who used the alternative term

"EQ" for the counterpart to IQ, the emotional quotient.

There is no communication without emotions. That means that conversational intelligence is emotional intelligence.

We cannot learn to have meaningful conversations unless we're willing to acknowledge, manage, and speak to the emotions that arise any time two people get together—professionally or personally. Being a charming person is not about making convincing arguments for how charming you are, but cultivating the emotions of connection and warmth. Likewise, conflict resolution and problem-solving aren't just a matter of being right or saying the most appropriate things—they're about understanding people and speaking to their emotional experience just as much as their practical one.

According to *Psychology Today*, emotional intelligence (EI) is "the *ability* to identify and manage one's own emotions as well as the emotions of others." So, it's an awareness that needs to go both ways. We all know about the power of listening, but we cannot be masterful listeners without first being skillful with our emotions and the emotions of others. We are all influenced by emotion—what varies is the degree to which we are aware of it and hence can control the process!

EI is a cluster of three separate skills, which we'll see popping up again and again:

1. Emotional **awareness** of self and others
2. The ability to **harness** and use emotions (hint: not suppress them!)
3. The ability to **manage** emotions (i.e., we always choose our actions no matter what)

Let's take a look at each one a little more closely.

Cultivating Emotional Awareness

If we are emotionally aware, we are able to identify what we are feeling in a conversation, as well as observe and comprehend what another person is feeling—even if it's wildly different from our own experience. Crucially, we are able to see a clear difference between our emotions and someone else's without getting confused. This explains why emotional awareness is a prerequisite for drawing healthy boundaries.

We have already begun to practice this in developing our body language reading skills—did you notice how posture, eye contact, proximity, etc. all reveal how the person in front of you *feels*? In good conversation, we are not merely seeking to understand the other person on a cognitive level (i.e., what they're *thinking*), but to feel what they feel and see what they see.

Actually, once you understand what someone feels, you may find it so much easier to understand what they think, anyway!

Emotional intelligence is realizing that the most important data that anyone can communicate with you at any time is what they are feeling—the factual content becomes a distant second. Imagine you're talking to someone, and you work hard to get your own prejudices, need for control, inflexibility, etc. out of the way so you can really observe this person. You see:

- A hunched posture with hands tightly curled in lap
- A low-volume voice but hurried and disorganized speech
- Gaze at the floor and hastily avoiding eye contact
- Corners of the mouth downturned, inner corners of eyebrows pinched toward center of forehead
- Frequent use of "I'm sorry" and phrases like, "I know this will sound stupid, but . . ."

Even if you completely ignore the verbal content of what you're told, emotional intelligence means putting all this together to see this person's sadness, low self-esteem, and perhaps anxiety. It is not rocket science to come to this conclusion—seeing it in bullet points like this makes it easy, right? But when you are out in the world and encountering real people, all this information may well be there . . . only you are not paying attention to it. Why? Because you're too busy with your own fears, opinions, and what you want to say next.

If you are emotionally aware, you may also notice that in this person's presence, you feel a subtle drop in your own energy levels. This is not magic; there is no intuition or gut feeling involved—you are simply **aware** of what is happening right before your eyes.

Now let's imagine that in this situation, the person in front of you is saying, "I'm feeling pretty positive about things these days, you know? This new job looks promising, and I think there's a lot of opportunity there. I know this will sound stupid, but isn't it strange how scary it can actually be to get what you want? I hoped and prayed I'd get this job, and now that I have it . . . it's, uh, it's really great. I guess."

If you "listened" only to the words, you'd miss so much of what this person was communicating. If you were emotionally intelligent, however, you would see a more nuanced view: perhaps because this person feels as though they *should* be happy about their new job, but they feel conflicted since they really aren't.

This brings up an important point about reading body language—we find meaning not in any single observation, gesture, or expression, but in the total sum of a person's behavior, in context, combined with everything else. So in this case, you might naturally wonder about the disparity between what is communicated verbally and what is communicated nonverbally. You realize that person only speaks this way when in the presence of a third person, but things change when they're alone with you. Why?

Become aware of all this and don't be surprised if people start believing that you have mind-reading powers! The better you understand what's going on with people—what's *really* going on—the faster you can establish rapport.

Develop this skill: The very next conversation you're in, quickly do a scan of both the other person and yourself, and see if you can settle on a single word or phrase to describe their current emotional experience in that conversation. If you find this difficult, keep it simple and ask just two questions:

Are they open or closed?
Are they advancing, retreating, or at rest?

Human behavior is pretty simple. When we're happy, we're open, we're responsive, and we move toward stimuli. When we're angry, we might advance, too, but in a completely different way. When we're sad or afraid, we do the opposite and retreat. Pretend you're a chimpanzee in the jungle and can't understand the words people are saying, but only read their most basic body language. Congratulations, you are now *more* perceptive than the average human! The more you practice quickly doing this in real time, the easier and more automatic it will become.

Harnessing Those Pesky Emotions

When you are unaware of emotions, you will necessarily be at their mercy. They will seem to you mysterious, unpredictable, and even annoying. **But when you are aware of emotions—yours and other people's—then you are in a position to proactively and consciously choose your response.** In our example, unless the person understands that they're feeling conflicted, they cannot take any steps to resolve the problem or choose something different. They will be pushed around by this sense of tension without ever knowing why or how it's happening.

Likewise, if you cannot be aware for them that this is happening, you are totally unable to understand where they're coming from and cannot even begin to be useful, empathetic, or supportive to them, because you don't actually know what they're experiencing or what they need.

So you smile broadly and shake their hand and congratulate them for their good fortune in securing such a great job. Any communication between the two of you is necessarily compromised because it lacks a foundation of real emotional awareness. Have you ever felt that some relationships have always seemed to remain shallow and unfulfilling somehow? Do you have people in your life where you think, "We never really *get* one another"? Chances are, there is a lack of emotional connection somewhere along the line.

With awareness, though, you can *harness* your experience and put it to use toward the things you consciously decide are important. For example, you can see your friend is struggling, and since you value being a good and empathetic friend, you can say kindly, "Hey, let me know if I've got this all wrong, but you seem a little unsure about this new job. How are you feeling about it?" The level of communication that is possible between the two of you is instantly enhanced. Now, it is possible to learn more about each other, to find solutions, to connect, and to leave a conversation saying, "That person really gets me."

How can you harness your own emotions or encourage others to harness theirs?

- **Frequently pause** during conversations and check in with yourself. How does your body, heart, and soul feel? Notice what your body is doing and what thoughts are in your mind. Notice what you're saying. There's no need for judgment or premature interpretation—just stop and do a little "awareness check" on what you're actually experiencing.
- You can invite someone else to do the same by **reflecting their experience** to heighten awareness. Describe what you're seeing and hearing. Put labels on emotions and experiences. "Hm, this seems like a *stressful* situation, huh?" or, "Do you think you're feeling a little *overwhelmed*?" Don't underestimate the power of simply asking, "Hey, how are you feeling right now?" You'd be surprised at how seldom some people actually pause and ask themselves this.
- In any conversation, you can gain control and awareness by **slowing down** (or pausing completely) and becoming aware. If you find yourself rushing, literally lean back and take a deep breath. You can still keep the conversation going

by asking an open-ended question rather than immediately responding.
- Finally, the essence of harnessing an emotion is learning to **use it**. In our example, the emotion of uncertainty and feeling conflicted can actually be a springboard for a really useful conversation about what is genuinely desired in a work role. It can also be an invitation to ramp up intimacy and connection with a friend—after all, it's only when we can honestly share our vulnerability with someone that we can develop trust and closeness. In this way, feelings that are acknowledged can be put to good use and help create connection, insight, or understanding.

Develop this skill: Once you've identified a word or phrase, see if it's possible to include them in the conversation somehow. This can be done even in low-key, superficial conversations—for example, "You seem a little unsure about what I've just said. What do you think?" or, "I'm not sure what I think about that yet. Can I get back to you?"

Emotional Management

For some people, the idea of managing emotions sounds wrong—isn't it a bad idea to try to suppress or deny how you actually feel? But think of emotions like any other biological urge—for example, hunger. You may be in the train station one day and feeling ravenous, and this is a legitimate and natural feeling that you don't need to deny or avoid. Nevertheless, you can manage that sensation by saying, "Oh well, there isn't anything to eat around here except overpriced junk food, so I'll wait an hour until I get home and have a healthy lunch there instead."

It's not that different with emotions. **We can accept and acknowledge how we feel with heaps of compassion and self-respect but at the same time make conscious choices about how we will behave regardless.**

Managing emotions is something you can do when you are able to maintain awareness of some higher goal. For example, if your higher goal is to ace an important job interview, it becomes necessary to down-manage your feelings of panic and self-doubt and deliberately seek to create feelings of calm. If you were listening to your friend talk about their fancy new job, and your goal was to be an excellent friend to them, you might choose to intentionally respond in ways that encourage empathy, connection, and closeness.

Being aware of and being able to harness and manage emotions may seem a little abstract and complicated, but it doesn't have to be. It all comes down to a shift in mindset:

- Shifting from being a slave of your emotions to being a master of them and using them as tools
- Shifting from being reactive to being intentional, deliberate, and conscious, i.e., making a choice
- Shifting from seeing emotions as secondary or irrelevant to communication, to seeing them as central

People like those who are emotionally intelligent. Those with high EQs have been said to be more effortless communicators and thrive not just in personal relationships but at work, too. In fact, it's hard to imagine a thing that wouldn't be improved with better emotional awareness and mastery.

Develop this skill: Now that you're aware of the emotion that you and the other person are feeling, ask how (or whether) you need to manage it. For example, if you can see that the other person is stressed, you might realize that it's worth saying something to soothe, reassure, or calm them down. Likewise, if you notice that you're angry, you might decide to ask for a time out so you can cool off and return to the conversation later.

Validation as Connection

Have you ever vented to someone about something that upset you, only to be told something like, "Come on, you're overreacting"? How did it make you feel to be told this? You probably felt awful, and that's unsurprising. Think about how it would feel if you said "109hat's a pretty red flower" and the other person said "It's not red—it's pink You're wrong."

You'd probably feel annoyed (you're not really asking for an argument about color, but to share your experience of the flower and how pretty it is) and also like you've said something bad or even that you're crazy. After all, it *looks* red to you. You still see red, and being told it's pink doesn't change that, right? Even more subtly, a new dynamic is introduced: The other person knows what is real, and *they* get to decide whether your judgment is sound or not. Annoying, isn't it?

If someone says "I'm scared" and the response they get is "You're not scared, don't be silly" or "You have no reason to be scared," it is exactly the same as being told that the color they clearly see as red is actually pink.

Validation is something we all seek when we communicate, whether we are conscious of the fact or not. Even if we're unconscious of our need to be validated, however, we know it feels bad to be *invalidated*!

Validation is simply the process of genuinely hearing, seeing, and witnessing another person's lived reality and allowing it to be what it is. When we validate something, we pay attention to it and affirm that what we observe is reasonable, legitimate, worthwhile, or **real** in some sense. Because of the powerful emotional component hidden in all human interaction, learning to truly validate someone is a potent tool to use in every conversation. If you consistently ensure that you are validating the people around you, all your conversations will feel deeper, more connected, and more harmonious.

Sadly, most of us completely misunderstand what validation really is. We might say things like, "Look I'm not trying to make you feel bad. It's just that the flower really is pink!" Again, when our own egos and preconceptions get in the way, we can focus on *that* instead of empathetically understanding what the other person really needs from us. Facts absolutely matter, but they are rarer than you think, and they are never the basis of a warm, connected interaction with someone.

What Validation ISN'T

To truly have empathy for someone and their position means to go beyond agreement or disagreement. When we validate someone by saying "that makes sense," we aren't saying that they are "right"—only that we can see that from their point of view, their reaction is rational and reasonable FOR THEM.

Imagine a conversation where someone is complaining about unfair treatment they have received at work. They are upset and feel attacked. The person hearing these complaints, though, goes immediately on a fact-finding mission in order to understand "what really happened." They may say things like, "Are you sure that's what they meant?" or, "You're probably blowing things out of proportion." It's all just different ways of saying, "I don't agree with your assessment." Which is just one way of saying, "You are wrong to feel what you feel," which on a deep emotional level will just be felt as "you, as a person, are wrong."

But really, if our goal in conversation is to connect and create intimacy, empathy, and shared understanding, then agreement is irrelevant. We don't have to have the same experience as the other person or agree with their interpretation to see that it's nevertheless the interpretation they have. People feel what they feel and experience what they experience. To be a good conversationalist, all you have to do is observe and acknowledge this for what it is. You are never required to weigh in, compare their experience against yours, or determine whether they are "allowed" to feel as they do given your assessment of the facts.

So, validation is not the same as agreement. However, it also doesn't mean reinforcement, either. Let's say someone is complaining bitterly about the treatment they receive at work, and the listener immediately grabs hold of those feelings of persecution and amplifies them. For example, they encourage a heavy conversation that goes on for two hours wherein every detail is dwelt on, encouraging the person to think of themselves as a wronged victim, continually drawing attention to the hurt and angry feelings. This may feel good in the short term, but it really only emphasizes negative emotions, and instead of finding useful ways to channel them, it exacerbates them.

Effective validation is simply the ability to communicate to someone: you are right to feel the way you feel. I witness you feeling that way and it makes sense. This is easier said than done since sometimes we can invalidate people precisely because we're trying so hard to make them feel better! For example:

"Cheer up, it could be worse!"
"Don't be silly!"
"Don't you worry, you'll be fine."
"Try to see the positives."
"Come on, don't say that."

All of the above are usually said by people who genuinely want to help. They may see, for example, that you are feeling down or anxious or angry. To validate this emotion would mean to say, "You are right to feel down/anxious/angry. I witness you feeling that way and it makes sense." This can be tricky to do because we look at their situation and disagree. If someone says, "I'm such a failure," our knee-jerk response might be to quickly blurt, "No, you're not! Don't say that!"

But if we do, we are actually invalidating them. You might think, "But how can I validate that they're a failure?" Well, you don't. Remember, it is irrelevant what the content is, and your agreement is not the point. *What you validate is their current emotional reality.* You are essentially saying, "I can see that you feel upset right now, and you have a right to feel what you feel." Whether they are "right" or "wrong" is beside the point—you could, after all, make a compelling argument for why they are not a failure, but it probably wouldn't change the fact that that is indeed how they feel.

Another example is when a small child says they're afraid of something. An adult can know for certain that there is nothing to be afraid of. But again, this is not what matters. Instead of saying, "Stop crying now. There's nothing to be afraid of," (which only tells the child that there is something wrong or unacceptable about how they feel), say, "I can see you're afraid. I know it's not nice to feel afraid. Would you like me to stay here with you?"

It is never wrong to have emotions. They simply are what they are. If we can only refrain from making people feel that their responses are wrong/mistaken/crazy/bad, then we are already halfway to validating them. Simply imagine that everyone you meet is in fact the world's leading expert on their own emotions. When it comes to lived experience, assume that everything someone tells you is indeed what is true for them—whether you can understand it personally or not.

Any time we call someone overly sensitive or illogical, or any time we suggest that there's a right way to feel—and they're not doing it, we are invalidating them. If we judge a person for the type, duration, or intensity of their emotion, we are invalidating them. For example:

"Wait, you don't want the job you just applied for? That's crazy." (Type)
"I can't believe you're *still* mad about that . . ." (Duration)
"Don't you think you're being a drama queen?" (Intensity)

Here, having enough emotional intelligence to identify and name people's emotions can be a wonderful way to validate them. You're not judging them or analyzing them but simply giving them a name.

"It seems like you're so scared right now."
"I can see that you're angry."
"It's understandable that you'd be really confused right now."

Merely to notice and observe genuine emotions are often validation enough, especially for people who are struggling to put their experience into words. Many people have been chronically invalidated all through life to the extent that they are not able to label their own feelings very well and will often feel bad without knowing why. If you can validate them and put a word to what they're feeling, you instantly convey a sense of compassion and empathy that is sorely missing in our world today. As you can imagine, to do this requires that we ourselves are comfortable with our own emotions—after all, how can we accept the feelings of others with compassion if we don't know how to do it for ourselves?

Finally, it's worth mentioning the phrase "I'd feel the same," or similar expressions. This can indeed be validating, but be careful. Like the phrase "I know how you feel" can feel hollow, validating someone's feelings by saying that they're the same as your own can backfire. If you genuinely would have thought/felt/acted the same way, then by all means say so—but it's usually more powerful to validate people simply because they feel how they feel—not because you just happen to agree with them.

Types of Validation

Broadly speaking, there are three types of validation:

1. Emotional
2. Behavioral
3. Cognitive

The type we offer will depend on the circumstances, the person in front of us and the overall purpose of the conversation. In some contexts, one type will be most appropriate, and in others, you might find that a blend of all three is needed.

1. Emotional Validation

Simply, this is to validate emotions without intensifying them. We do this by **centering and focusing on the other person's feelings without judgment, interpretation, or analysis.** Something to bear in mind is that emotions can be layered, and they are dynamic, which means they move and change over time.

As you develop your own emotional awareness, you may start to notice the difference between primary and secondary emotions. For example, someone may appear to be consumed with rage, but this is really a secondary emotion; underneath the rage is intense sadness and upset, the primary emotion. **We can understand secondary emotions to be our feelings about our feelings.** So, someone may experience a devastating loss and sink into feelings of sadness. But if they feel that this sadness is too threatening to experience fully, and they don't accept that emotion as legitimate (i.e., they invalidate themselves!), then they may respond to their own sadness with rage.

If you are astute, you can see the rage and validate it but also see beyond it and validate the hidden primary emotion. As you can imagine, when you are able to compassionately validate something in someone else that they themselves are still struggling to accept, you create powerful feelings of trust and connection and make an opportunity for that emotion to be transformed and released. In this example, helping someone acknowledge the deeper hurt they really feel—and come to terms with that—will help dissolve their rage. Again, we see how emotional awareness is all about our ability to harness and manage emotions once we've become aware of them. It can also help us recognize when, to put it bluntly, *it's not about us*!

2. Behavioral Validation

This is when we communicate that another person's *actions* are understood regardless of whether or not they are beneficial or something that we ourselves would have done. Indirectly, this also creates a feeling of emotional validation, but it's a form of support and empathy that may be more appropriate for the workplace.

For example, "It makes sense that you would shut yourself away and hermit for a while after what happened," or, "I can totally see why you did that." Simply restating the facts of a situation without adding any of your own analysis or interpretation can actually be a kind of behavioral validation too. It's like you're saying, "Yup, this happened. It is what it is," without trying to turn that action into something.

Behavioral validation can be a good tool to use when someone has actually made a mistake. You validate them not to say that what they did was right, but that you can recognize how they made the decision to act that way regardless. Behavioral validation can express that you respect and understand why someone chose to act as they did, even if the outcome isn't what you or they wanted.

So, for example, when giving critical feedback: "I can see why you chose to resolve the complaint in the way you did (validating the behavior), and it made sense to do it that way. I can also tell that this has been very upsetting for you (emotional validation). However, seeing how things have escalated, it's clear we need to try a different approach going forward (the crux of the feedback).

Often, stalemates can be shifted and resolutions found if you can validate the *effort* and *intention* behind an action, even if the action itself isn't great. "I really love how much thought you put into this gift, and I know you wanted to surprise me, but I'm afraid it doesn't fit and I'm going to have to return it."

3. Cognitive Validation

Cognitive validation occurs when one acknowledges and names the underlying assumptions and ideas held by another person and then helps that person articulate those thoughts so they can validate them themselves. This is a little different from the previous two and is most commonly used in certain forms of counseling and therapy.

We can use the overall principle in everyday life whenever we validate somebody's thought processes. Often, people will actively seek cognitive validation when they've come to a conclusion and want to know that they're not crazy for doing so. They want others to reflect back that they have correctly appraised a situation and that their thoughts are rational and make sense.

For example, the same friend mentioned earlier might come to you and share that they are struggling with the decision to accept their recent job offer or turn it down:
"I think I need to turn it down because on second thought, I just know it's not right for me..." They may talk at length about their reasons—i.e., their thoughts, evaluations, and interpretations of the situation—and in doing so, they are seeking confirmation that this cognitive process is sound.

Again, this is tricky—you are not required to say what *you* would do in the situation, nor give your advice according to your own values. Let's say they explain how although the pay is better, the commute is longer, and overall, they would be making less. They've decided, mentally, that the new job is not worth it, and you can validate this by saying, "Hm, yeah, I can see that. You've weighed it all up, and it seems like you're coming to the same conclusion each time."

Notice here that it's not the content of the thought processes that are being validated or not—but the processes themselves. Since obviously this can get tricky, you might find that it's really helpful simply to say, "I can tell that you've given this a lot of thought," and actively inquire about the values, principles, and worldview that would help that person feel more confident in their assessment and the decision they'll make.

You might ask, "Do you think you ultimately value more money or more free time at this point in your career?" and this could help them explore and validate their own cognitive process without you ever having to share your own opinion on the matter. Counselors who work with victims of abuse frequently use this approach, too: "You did what you had to in order to survive, and whatever that was, was right at the time." This is so they can create empowerment and responsibility and help people extricate themselves from abusive dynamics, but without falling into self-blame for not preventing what has already happened. Essentially, it is cognitive validation, because it's saying "You can trust yourself and your thought processes."

Naturally, these three types of validation can blend into one another and be offered all at once. For example, "Wow, I can see how stressed this has made you! (Emotional validation.) It's no wonder you've asked for a few days off. (Behavioral validation.) It makes sense that you took a breather before you got completely burnt out. (Cognitive validation.)"

Acceptance and the Six Levels of Listening

Now that we've learned a little about validation and the importance of emotional intelligence, we can move on to what is arguably *the* communication skill—listening.

Listening is not passive. When we listen, we are not simply being quiet and "allowing" the other person to talk. Rather, good listening is an attitude we take to information that is shared with us. **It's the ability to be open and receptive, to accept what we're told, but also to process and really engage with that**

information so that we can also return it to the speaker if appropriate.

The skill of listening is a little like the skill of driving; everyone thinks they're better than average at it even though this is a statistical improbability! In *Listening to Conflict*, author Eric Van Slyke outlines six listening levels. The reason he breaks it down is that not every situation requires your full-blown attention and devotion, but on the other hand, sometimes "good" listening can be "great" listening if it's only dialed up a notch. Let's take a look at the levels with an example to illustrate.

Level 1: Passive listening
This is barely what most people would consider listening at all. The "listener" is sort of vaguely aware that the speaker is talking, and they are quiet, but there is very little entering into the listener's conscious awareness. You've probably experienced this yourself—if you suddenly ask the listener what they think, they might reply, "Huh? About what?"

Level 2: Responsive listening
The next level up is where we do some passive listening but also give occasional verbal and nonverbal cues that we are in fact paying attention. Our comprehension is still limited, though, because we are mostly just giving the

impression of listening by saying things like "uh huh" when we think we should.

Level 3: Selective listening
At this level, we are actually starting to pay attention, but it's not complete attention to the entirety of the message. We may pick out words that appeal specifically to us—for example, our own names or some topic in which we are personally interested—and kind of ignore the rest.

Level 4: Attentive listening
One up from selective listening is attentive listening, where we might start to show signs of engaging with material being shared with us. We might ask questions or try to clarify details because we're actively processing the message.

Now, the reasons we are doing this could be extremely varied. We might be paying attention purely because we are nosy, or because we're trying to extract some juicy gossip! Whatever it is, we're not exclusively trying to listen for the other person's benefit, but because we would like to know what they know. In other words, attentiveness alone does not imply understanding or empathy, but it's a necessary starting point for them!

Level 5: Active listening

At this level, we begin to care about listening for emotional content. We are not just hearing the factual details of the message being shared, but we're gaining a deeper comprehension of what those details mean, particular to the speaker, and how they fit into the bigger picture. At this level, we are giving more consistent nonverbal feedback and asking questions that show we're really engaging with the story, often being able to process and add information before passing it back. There may be a subtle shift where we are not only listening for our own benefit, but can start to also see the value in the other person's story simply because it has value for them.

Level 6: Empathic listening
At this level, things go even deeper still, and we begin not only to see the emotional content from our perspective but the emotional content as it is seen by the other person. This is the root of empathy and real compassion. We are able to suspend our own view on things and see through the eyes of the listener. Crucially, we do this without judgment. When we are empathic, we are deeply connected to another person and their experience and may often feel moved enough to help them in some way. If communication reaches this level, healing transformations, deep understandings, and feelings of love and belonging are possible.

So, what level is "best"? Well, the answer to that is the one that the other person most needs from you in any given context. Attentive and active listening are both great levels to aim for in everyday interpersonal connections, whereas we can strive for more empathetic listening for those closest to us or situations where the other person is reaching out in distress or needs our *full* attention, empathy, and witness.

It would be a mistake to think that full-on empathetic listening is the gold standard and something to aim for in every interaction. That will quickly overwhelm and alienate people. Rather, it's about pitching your listening level to match what is being shared, how it's being shared, and in what context.

To be a good listener, try to remember H-U-R:

- **H**earing the Message
- **U**nderstanding the message
- **R**esponding to the message

Hearing the Message

It sounds obvious, but the first step is to really, truly want to listen and to hear the other person. That's not the same as feeling an ego boost at the idea of yourself as a good listener—it means actually being a good listener! Every human being is fascinating if you will only listen. Be curious and ask questions—not with the intention to appraise or argue or compare or judge, but just to learn.

As we've already seen, removing psychological barriers and working on emotional intelligence will mean you are more *present* in the conversation and therefore able to receive what is being shared with you. Listen with the intent to understand only—which means forgetting for a moment that you are going to speak when they are done. Don't look at your phone and don't let your gaze get caught by people passing or events just outside the frame. For this moment, the other person is your world. What do you want to know?

Bearing in mind what you know about body language and nonverbal communication, listen with your own body. Any time two people get together to communicate, their bodies encounter one another—what is their body saying to yours?

If you have had some practice becoming aware of, harnessing, and managing your own emotions, you can bring that attitude to the conversation. Be neutral, be patient, and be conscious. Keep asking yourself about the emotional content being shared, and *accept* it without judgment or interpretation. When we let go of the need to rush, pass judgment, or quickly grasp for a solution (i.e., our need for control), then we can do something far more interesting: fully immerse in the perspective of the other person.

To listen well, you never have to be a mind reader. You don't have to turn into some near-psychic counselor figure who intuits what's going on. Instead, if you don't quite understand, ask! This neatly leads us to . . .

Understand the Message

You may have noticed that people don't always say what they mean, or mean what they say. The person you're talking to may be exquisitely self-aware, or they may be confused and present you a jumbled, almost incoherent message.

As a dedicated and self-aware listener, you have a few jobs:

1. Seek clarification if you don't understand something
2. Confirm that you have actually understood by paraphrasing or reflecting
3. Make sure you have correctly heard the emotional content of the message

For example, consider this short exchange:

A: I was so shocked, I think I nearly died!

B: *Died*? Wait, do you mean die because you were really unhappy with what happened . . . ?
A: Oh no, I mean that I was so thrilled and happy it nearly bowled me over, you know?
B: Oh, totally, I get it. You were excited! You were knocked right off your feet, huh?
A: Uh huh, and I just did not know what to do with myself, let me tell you . . .

In the above, Person B doesn't make any assumptions and quickly clarifies with a neutral and non-judgmental question. Then, they confirm their understanding of the emotional content by immediately labeling the emotion they observe (excitement) and further reflecting that understanding by using another metaphor that's somewhat in line with the one used by Person A, i.e., being bowled over, being knocked off your feet.

You never need to worry about asking people clarifying questions—these will usually only show that you're paying attention and that you care about getting the details right. Far better to ask early on so that later in the conversation, you don't come across as having not paid attention or completely got the wrong end of the stick. Use phrases like:

"Can I just ask . . ."
"It seems like XYZ . . . Have I got that right?"
"Have I understood?"

"Can you help me understand XYZ . . . ?"

Respond to the Message

There are three basic ways to respond to what you've been told: paraphrase, reflect, and summarize (it's possible to do all three at once!). When you paraphrase, you repeat the message you've heard but in your own words to show that the message has reached you and that you comprehend the gist of it. Even making small encouraging sounds like "uh huh" and "oh?" as you listen will help. Reflecting is similar, but we may mirror the emotional content too. Summarizing is about taking what we've heard, listening for the essence, and returning this condensed essence back to the speaker.

Don't underestimate the power of summarizing—it may not seem like a valuable thing to do, but it will instantly communicate that you've heard, you've understood, and you've even been able to process it all. For some people, simply hearing a condensed version of their current situation reflected to them is validation enough and can lead to mental shifts that help with problem-solving and breakthroughs in creativity.

But responding is not limited to what you do in that immediate moment. It is even more powerful if you can absorb the message, process it, and return with a considered response long after the end of that conversation. If you can refer to a previous conversation and tie in what you heard then with what you're hearing now, the other person will likely feel deeply acknowledged and heard. This will foster valuable feelings of trust and familiarity over time.

If you can consistently hear, understand, and respond to the messages people share with you, the foundations for good listening are in place—and that applies whether you are listening at level 3 or at level 6. Take a look at the following conversation and see how the skills of reflecting, summarizing, paraphrasing, validating, asking questions, pausing occasionally, and naming emotions help the speaker feel heard and understood. This is a conversation held at level 6 between close friends, but the same principles apply with any conversation.

A: This breakup could not have come at a worse time, and to be honest, I just feel like everything in my world is crumbling (hunched over, tense body language, and voice low and quivering).
B: Wow (leaning in and matching body language and voice, pausing).
A: What am I going to do? We've just signed a lease together. It's a nightmare.
B: I'm so sorry (pausing again as though to invite the other person to speak more).

A: Ugh, I'm such a mess right now. I've been up crying all night. It's so embarrassing!

B: No, not embarrassing at all! It makes perfect sense you'd feel that way (acceptance and emotional validation).

A: I guess I just feel so stupid because this really felt like the one, you know? I realize we weren't together all that long..."

B: No? Can you just remind me how long you were together for? (Clarification question).

A: It was about a year and a half, two years. The funny thing is, I'm surprised at how relieved I am, in a way.

B: Relieved? (Simply repeating the key emotional word here to reflect and mirror).

A: Yeah. I don't know, it doesn't even make sense to me, but I'm glad he's gone and also completely devastated he's gone, you know?

B: It's like it's something you wanted... but that doesn't mean it doesn't hurt (summarizing and paraphrasing).

A: Exactly. But then at some moments, like last night, I get second thoughts and I start doubting myself, I don't know. I just don't know what I think.

B: Oh man. It sounds like this is a pretty confusing time for you right now (naming the emotion).

A: Exactly!

Now take a look at the very same conversation again and see if you can identify where Person B has failed to listen properly.

A: This breakup could not have come at a worse time, and to be honest, I just feel like everything in my world is crumbling (hunched over, tense body language, and voice low and quivering).
B: Oh my God, men! (Voice raised, tone irritated, and body language expansive and energetic).
A: Yeah. Plus, we signed a lease together just the other day, so it really feels like such a nightmare.
B: Wait, what? You signed a lease together? Oh boy...
A: I know! I now feel like such an idiot. Last night, all I could think about was—
B: You need to get out of that lease, whatever you do. Can you chat with the landlord or something? There's got to be a way.
A: Well, uh, I guess. I haven't thought of that yet.
B: The exact same thing happened to me years ago. I sorted it out with the landlord, and he understood. Easy peasy. But you have to get it fixed *now*.
A: Yeah. You're right. Uh, thanks.
B: Sure, no problem. No point getting angry, right? Just do what you need to do (laughing).

In this conversation, B begins by failing to be aware of or match A's nonverbal communication or body language, and then responds immediately with judgment. When A starts to speak again, B interrupts with forceful advice that brings the conversation to a screeching halt—and leaves A feeling exposed and vulnerable since the response is practical and pragmatic and doesn't acknowledge the emotional content at all. Finally, B mentions themselves and their own experiences and casually dismisses A's perspective (almost as though to say, "I didn't find this a problem personally, so you shouldn't either!"). The cherry on top is when B incorrectly labels the emotion they guess A to be experiencing (anger), which likely leaves A feeling completely unheard and unsupported. Person B may sincerely believe that they've been helpful and positive, but the effect is the opposite—Person A may feel even worse than they did to start.

Summary:

- There is no communication without emotions. That means that conversational intelligence is emotional intelligence. EQ is a mix of three skills: awareness of emotions, harnessing emotions, and managing emotions.
- If we are emotionally aware, we are able to identify what we are feeling in a conversation as well as observe and comprehend what another person is feeling—even if it's wildly different from our own experience. We are also then in a

position to harness those emotions and to proactively and consciously choose a response.

- Slow down or pause, reflect what you're being told, and see if you can put the newly identified and named emotion to good use.
- Managing emotions means being conscious and deliberate: We can accept and acknowledge how we feel but still make conscious choices about our behavior according to our chosen goals.
- Validation is the process of genuinely hearing, seeing, and witnessing another person's lived reality and allowing it to be what it is. It's crucial in good communication. Validation is not agreement or reinforcement but recognizing emotions for what they are. It can be emotional, behavioral, or cognitive—or all three.
- Good listening is the ability to be open and receptive, to accept what we're told, but also to process and really engage with that information so that we can also return it to the speaker if appropriate.
- There are six increasing levels of listening: passive, responsive, selective, attentive, active, and empathic. Remember your role as a listener with the HUR acronym: **h**ear the message, **u**nderstand it, and **r**espond. We can respond and show our understanding by paraphrasing, reflecting, and summarizing.

Chapter 4. As If It Wasn't Hard Enough…

So far, we've seen what it takes to have a broadly pleasant conversation (remove psychological barriers, pay attention to body language, use the rule of three), and by using just these tools, we can be sure of having great interactions with others. But what happens when things don't work out so well and you need to navigate a difficult, emotionally upsetting conversation or manage conflict?

During the heat of the moment, a difficult conversation can make us forget every nice-sounding skill and technique we've ever learned and start to respond with defensiveness, fear, judgment, or even aggression—all of which we have seen create fertile ground for miscommunication and hostility.

In subtle (or not so subtle!) ways, we can start to feel like they are our enemy, and whatever they say becomes something to defend against—i.e., to shut down immediately. The purpose of the conversation shifts to defense, attack, or a mix of both, and instead of looking for things to agree on, we seize things that are causing problems, and amplify them.

Below, we will look at two powerful frameworks to maintain connected communication even during tricky situations. Each of them succeeds, however, because they do one thing: increase positivity and decrease feelings of defensiveness and fear.

During a conflict, we may feel that our only aim is to make our point, be vindicated, or place blame. But really, **our aim should be completely different: to increase positive feelings for everyone involved.** Only *then* do we have any hope of actually being heard, validated, or respected.

Let's look at a tricky situation and how we can use these two frameworks to help us create more feelings of positivity.

The COIN Framework

It's tempting to imagine that other people think as we do, want what we want, and see the world in roughly the same way as we see it. But if you've ever been in any conflict, you'll know what a rude awakening it can be to realize that another person's mind can be a whole universe of its own. With assumptions, shortcuts, and lazy language, we can mutually lull one another into feeling that we have actually connected and understood—when we've done nothing of the sort.

Even if someone is very close to us and we know them well, they are going to be coming at any situation or problem from a completely unique background, with a different identity, set of expectations, and interpretations. We are always communicating across different identities, lived experiences, biases, and priorities.

The COIN framework is a tool you can use to get a handle on all this (that includes everything YOU bring to the table, too), interrupt bias and assumption, and clear away misunderstandings and confusion. Created by executive coach Anna Carroll in 2003, this model was originally about giving feedback in the workplace, but it's now used in many other contexts, too. In Carroll's book, *The Feedback Imperative: How to Give Feedback to Speed Up Your Team's Success*, she explains a simple method for organizing difficult or emotional conversations.

While the framework might seem a little awkward and uncomfortable at first, it's probably a lot less uncomfortable than getting into full-blown conflict, and it does get better with time.

The framework goes like this:

C – Context – What has actually happened? What is the context, i.e., when and where and how did this event come to be? More than that, how are your own values and actions playing into it all?

O – Observation – Identify your assumptions, observations, thoughts, and beliefs about the context above. Importantly, this is done neutrally—without judgment, analysis, or interpretation. If possible, imagine you are a third party trying to simply describe what is happening.

I – Impact – What has been the overall impact on you? Why exactly are you concerned about this situation? However, this is not just the impact on you, but on others and the entire situation—so how are your actions influencing others and affecting things in turn?

N – Next – This is a request for something to change. It's you sharing your desired results and exploring potential options and opportunities so that some kind of resolution or agreement can be found.

Okay, so how can we put this all into practice? First, a COIN conversation is best understood as something that you prepare carefully for in advance. This is a tool for those tricky conflicts that are ongoing and require a choice or decision from you. Whether it's at work or in a personal context, take a moment to think about the situation on your own first, and then respectfully reach out to the other party, explaining that you'd like to start a conversation. Be willing to be turned down and be open to scheduling a conversation in a way that suits them most.

The framework is useful for emergencies, but it never hurts to approach any difficult conversation with a spirit of curiosity, collaboration, and respect. Let's look at an example to see how the whole process may play out. Imagine that two sisters are having a recurrent disagreement that's now reached crisis point. Sister A feels like Sister B continually makes heavy demands on her, which she bends over backward to accommodate, only for Sister B to cancel plans last minute and leave her sister hanging in a flurry of confusion. This has led to Sister A being unwilling to accommodate any further requests, and Sister B feeling that this is rude and hostile behavior.

Sister A decides that things are deteriorating and some honest communication is called for. On a day when she knows her sister will not be too distracted or busy, she sends her a text message asking if they can both sit down and have a good chat. This is agreed, and they both have time to process and think carefully about what they'd like to say.

Sister A: "Thanks for agreeing to chat with me, Sister B. I know you're busy at the moment with XYZ. I wanted to talk to you about some difficulty I've been having with the dynamic we seem to have lately. I want to clear things up, though, because you're my sister and I love you, and I know we can be such a good team when we connect well. Speaking to you about this is a little nerve-wracking, so please bear with me. I wanted to first just tell you how I saw things and tell you my perspective so you can see where I'm coming from. Then I wanted to ask you for your honest perspective, too. Do you think you have, like, twenty minutes to hash this out with me? We can put a pin in this and return to it whenever would work for you best."

Sister B: "Well, okay. Let's just talk now. I have time."

Sister A: "Okay, that's great, I'm happy to hear that. So, to be more specific, from what I can see, the last three times you've asked me to keep a weekend clear for you so we can do something together, you actually ended up cancelling on me at the last minute. The weekend before last, in particular, I drove out to meet you as we agreed, and you only told me an hour *after* we were due to meet that you could no longer make the meeting. Do you remember that weekend?"

Sister B: "Yeah, of course I do."

Sister A: "Okay, great. Well, this last weekend, you got in touch and wanted to meet again, but this time I said I was busy."

Sister B: "Well, I remember that too . . . I desperately needed your help, and you weren't there for me."

Sister A: "I understand. I'm really interested to hear your perspective on events, but I wanted to first share how things looked from my point of view so you can see my perspective too. What do you think?"

Sister B: "Okay, fine. Sorry. Please continue."

Sister A: "Cancelling on me three times in a row like that made me feel like I wasn't important to you, and I also felt pretty angry, like my time was not as important as yours. It really had a bad impact on me because it's time that is wasted that I can't get back. I also worry that it damages trust between you and me, and I don't like feeling as though I can't rely on you."

Sister B: (sighing) "Yeah, I'm sorry, I do get that . . ."

Sister A: "I know things have been pretty tense and awkward between us. Has that been your experience, too?"

Sister B: "Yup."

Sister A: "I value our relationship so much—you know I do! I always want to be there for you, and I also want to know that if you give me your word, I can rely on it. I want to ask you if you can think carefully about the next time we make plans, and that you don't agree to do anything unless you one hundred percent fully intend to follow through. I want us to both agree on that. That way we can both depend a little more on each other and can get rid of some of this awkwardness and confusion.

Sister B: "I agree. You're right and I'm sorry. I've been a little difficult lately, I know . . ."

And so on. Now, you might notice a few things in reading the above conversation. First, yes, it's a bit stilted and unnatural sounding. If you try to use the COIN approach on a loved one, they *will* notice the carefully deliberate language—and that's okay. Though it's awkward, it still works, and it sends a subtle message along the lines of, "this conversation is different from the kinds of interaction we've had so far. I mean this and I intend to take this problem seriously." You'd be surprised how conveying this attitude alone can actually put people in a receptive, respectful frame of mind—even while there is plenty of awkwardness.

A second thing you might notice is that, in real life, the process will not move in a neat, linear fashion from one step to the next. There needs to be a little flexibility in how the method is deployed, and context, observation, impact, and next may overlap considerably. That's also okay. You might find that the conversation takes on a complete life of its own—but if you have prepared yourself beforehand and have explored each point thoroughly, then you are able to express yourself effectively without running through the acronym in your mind. This will make things feel a little more natural.

A few things to bear in mind with the COIN framework:

- As much as possible, try to **use "I" statements** and focus on your perceptions, your feelings, your thoughts—not just grammatically but also in spirit. For example, "I feel that you're a big idiot" is not going to get you far!
- **Frequently pause** during the conversation to confirm that your observations are correct/reasonable.

The more you can have the other person agree with you (even if it's only on superficial details like the date an event happened), the more they are primed to collaborate with you in other ways. Create opportunities for them to concur with you.

- When making a request, **be clear, direct, and simple**. You want to decrease chances for misunderstanding but also present your needs and wants without arousing defensiveness. In the above conversation, Sister A makes a point of saying "I want us both to agree on that" to emphasize that she is not making a demand, but requesting a joint collaboration for their mutual benefit. Nevertheless, she's being pretty clear: don't stand me up again!
- **Don't keep repeating yourself.** Once ground has been covered and you have been heard, don't return to the same grievance over and over. Be careful about how you phrase your observations, etc., say them assertively but with kindness, and then drop it, making space for the other person to respond.
- **Remember your non-verbal body language** and maintain eye contact, keep an open posture, regulate your voice, and use inviting, open-handed gestures.

- Finally, bear in mind that **the conversation may still fail**. It's a sad fact that even if you do your very best to make your case and express yourself with clarity and respect, the situation may still worsen. Try to detach yourself from the outcome and make it your goal simply to act within your own integrity and express yourself as clearly and kindly as possible. Beyond that, let it go. Making a request will drastically increase your chances of having it granted—but it's never a guarantee.

At some point in life, most of us will have to communicate to someone about what they did or said, with the intention of encouraging or reducing that behavior, whether that's in a professional or personal context. Here, the COIN framework really shines:

Focus on the "Next" section and pay attention to what can be done in the future rather than dwelling on what hasn't been done in the past. For example, instead of saying, "The report was too long," you could say, "Next time, you could try making the report a lot shorter."

Use the COIN acronyms, but remember to include the positive behavior, too, and the impact it had. When you include observations followed by impact, you are essentially telling people *why* their behavior was positive or negative. You are not just complaining by showing consequences. This way, both you and the person are standing outside of their performance and looking in. As long as you approach any feedback conversation (including where you receive feedback!) with the same spirit of collaboration, it can be an effective and fruitful way to connect with someone.

How to Say No

Speaking of conflict, isn't "no" the epitome?

For people who have difficulty saying no, the word seems to be associated only with things like rudeness, violence, or stubbornness. They see no as a word that kids use during tantrums, or something that's said when someone is trying to be difficult. But no is a word we use to assert boundaries, and there are in fact many different shades and nuances to the practice of asserting ourselves—if we want to become masters at being assertive, we need to be familiar with each one.

Basic assertion is when you simply state your need, preference, limit, or personal belief:

"My budget for this is five hundred dollars."

"I'm not happy with the service I've received."

"I'm celiac and can't eat that."

"I'm really upset right now."

Basic assertions are when we state facts or express ourselves within our rights. We are most effective at making basic assertions when we keep things *simple* and *neutral*. We don't have to beg, plead, explain, justify, or apologize. It doesn't only have to be factual, however. We can state how we feel, but remember to use "I" statements to own your feelings, i.e. say, "I don't think this looks good," vs. "This is hideous." For some people, taking responsibility for how they feel, what they believe, what they want and don't want, and their limits is enormously empowering in itself. Sometimes, it can be hard just to speak up and make these things known. For example, if someone keeps offering you food, it's a basic assertion to say calmly, "Thank you, but I'm watching my weight and don't want any more."

Finally, a clever way to indirectly make a basic assertion is to say, "What would you like me to deprioritize?" when your boss heaps yet another task on your plate, for example. This way, you are communicating the message, "I can only do so many things at once—which things should they be?" You assert your boundary without being inflexible, and make it the other person's job to reconcile the overload, not yours.

An **empathic assertion** is a little different, in that it is designed to take into account the other person's feelings, needs, and wants, even as you state your own. This is especially important to master if you buy into the "saying no means I don't care" counter-mindset. Using empathic assertions shows the other person that you are asserting your boundary while you acknowledge and are sensitive to their position, too.

"I know that you were really hoping for a better outcome. I'm afraid this is the result for now, however."

"I understand that you're overwhelmed with this project. I nevertheless have to ask that you take these issues to the right channels from now on."

"I'm sure you haven't had an easy time lately. I still need you to fulfil your duties on this project as we agreed."

We can use this kind of assertion in many ways. We can use it to ask for extra help and consideration ourselves, but also we can use it to turn down the request for extra help and consideration when we can't give it. Sometimes, saying no and asserting boundaries does inconvenience or disappoint people, but that doesn't mean we can't express our regret and compassion.

Notice that in the above expressions, we avoid following the empathic statement with "but," which would only end up canceling out any feelings of compassion and even come across as passive-aggressive. For example, "I see your point, but..." may only come across as insincere or dismissive. Instead, try to use "and" or soften the sentences so you're not undermining the empathy you're expressing.

A **consequence assertion** is, hopefully, not something you have to do all that often. If we set healthy boundaries, communicate them, and assert them when people threaten to overstep, we will seldom need to make this kind of assertion. But occasionally, we need to follow up with consequences when someone violates our boundaries or is aggressive, and we want to respond without becoming aggressive ourselves.

The key here is to keep aggression and strong emotion out of it. Keep your voice calm, your tone neutral, and your body language relaxed. A boundary, remember, is a kind of conditional, i.e. "If X, then Y." To assert this is not to make a threat or ultimatum, but merely to state a fact.

"If you talk to me like that again, I'm going to end the conversation and take some time to reconsider this relationship."

"I'm afraid I'm not willing to keep taking part in this project until the safety concerns that have been raised are properly addressed."

"If this behavior doesn't change, I will have no choice but to get your supervisor involved."

Importantly, consequence assertions are a last resort, and come after gentle boundary assertions have been ignored. The thing is, a boundary isn't worth much unless it's actually enforced and there are real consequences for it being violated. Though this kind of "ultimatum" can be hard to deliver, you may be surprised by how strong you feel afterward. Don't make this kind of assertion unless you actually have consequences to deliver and are genuinely willing to follow through with them.

A **discrepancy assertion** is something you might need to make well before a consequence assertion is necessary. This is simply you pointing out the difference between what was agreed on and what is actually occurring, i.e. there's a misunderstanding, contradiction, or broken promise.

"We agreed last week that I'd have the final say when it comes to the budget, but now you're asking for a second opinion on these figures. Can you clarify that that is in fact what we agreed?"

"When we signed up for that marathon, you promised me you'd train with me every other day, rain or shine, remember?"

A discrepancy assertion gives the other party time to respect the agreement or back off from a boundary by reminding them that it's there and that you will not tolerate having it pushed back little by little!

Negative feelings assertions are needed when you want to express the emotional impact someone's behavior is having on you. This is not to blame them or make them responsible, but to make them aware of their effect on you and give them time to change. Start by describing their behavior as objectively and calmly as possible, and then clearly explain the impact on you without making sweeping generalizations or judgments. Describe how you feel and then end with an explanation of what specifically you would like them to do.

Don't say, "You never go to sleep when you should and you keep me up all night, and you make me so groggy in the morning. It sucks."

Say, "When you come to bed late, it makes it difficult for me to get sleep. I end up feeling really exhausted in the mornings. I'd really appreciate if you could make an effort to come to bed on time in the future, as we agreed."

As you practice the above, another thing to keep in mind is that you may need to repeat yourself (except if it's a consequence assertion, in which case you should be prepared to follow through if the boundary is still not respected after that). Try the "broken record" technique where you simply repeat yourself calmly and neutrally over and over. This is a good thing to practice since people who would erode your boundaries often tend to do it by degree, pushing a bit at a time, hoping that your no will gradually become a yes.

How to Communicate When You Don't Agree

Dale Carnegie put it best when he once said, "You can't win an argument. You can't because if you lose it, you lose it; and if you win it, you lose it." This is the spirit with which we'll approach all three of the following techniques.

Technique 1: The Agreement Frame

The agreement frame offers a straightforward method of communication that makes it easier for you to convey your viewpoint or a potential solution to the problem. **It helps the other person release their resistance to your perspective because you are able to really support *their* views or values, while at the same time offering them a new choice to take into consideration—yours.** There can be no conflict when there is no resistance. So with that logic, one way to avoid conflict is to lead in such a way that there is as little resistance as possible. Enter the technique called "the agreement frame."

This is basically a way to present yourself and your message as fundamentally in agreement with the other person's. Whether it is or isn't is not the point—you are framing it as though it were. The main principle is to use the words **"yes, and" rather than "yes, but."** It's simple but extremely effective. When people hear "but," they hear opposition and resistance. It may be slight and unconscious, but internally, they will gear up to push back against you, or else they will perceive that you are positioning yourself against them.

The agreement frame is a different approach. Let's say your spouse says to you, "The priority right now is to save money, not spend it on expensive gifts for family." Imagine you disagree with this and are trying to communicate toward some kind of compromise without arousing defensiveness or resistance. Instead of saying, "Yes, but we can still save a little and make sure we get people Christmas presents," you say, "Yes, and we can still save a little and make sure we get people Christmas presents."

It's a small change that makes all the difference in the world. Essentially, you are framing your position as one of alignment. If someone perceived that you're broadly on the same "side" as them, there is nothing to argue about. In this example, wanting to save money and wanting to spend it on Christmas presents for relatives is not set up as a fundamental war. Rather, the two ideas are put together, and the "yes, and" between them expresses that they can comfortably exist in the same universe.

You might be thinking surely this isn't enough to magically dissolve all conflict? After all, there is only a fixed amount of money, and at some point or another, you have to decide to put it toward *either* presents or savings, right? While this is true, the fact is that so long as you perceive your position and the other person's position as opposites, conflict is inevitable. It is only when you can start to conceive of both positions as compatible that you can begin to think about creative solutions, compromises, and ways forward. In this example, it may be that the solution to the conflict is to do a bit of both: save some money but still buy small-ish gifts for family.

Here are a few other phrases you can use to create an agreement frame:

- "I respect . . . and . . ."
- "I appreciate . . . and . . ."
- "I agree with . . . and . . ."

You might find it valuable to literally say, "I'm on your side here," or, "Let's figure this out together." Simply using language that puts you and the other person in agreement somehow will remove resistance and friction enough so that you can start seeing solutions.

A variation on this approach is called the Ransberger Pivot. This is a principle that allows conflict, once it already exists, to come to a fruitful conclusion. It is a method of communication that was first popularized by Ray Ransberger and Marshall Fritz in 1982. This method is not unlike the agreement frame since the goal is to find things that both sides can agree on. Here's how it's done:

1. **Listen** attentively and try to discern the values and emotions behind what is being said
2. **Voice agreement** means identifying something in their message that you have in common
3. **Admit misunderstanding**, own up to mistakes, and frame conflict as a temporary setback that you are both moving on from

For example, you have a complaint from a customer and begin simply by hearing their side of things without interrupting or rushing them. To clarify and show that you're paying attention, you might even ask clarifying questions like, "What makes this important to you?" and, "Can you tell me more about how you're feeling about XYZ?"

Next, once you've heard the underlying emotions, values, and needs, address them by finding some point of agreement. You might say, "I know you're disappointed in the quality of the service you received. I'm the same way—I hate feeling like a company has been careless about things," or, "It's clear to me that we both care deeply about resolving this fairly."

As you continue to talk, move to the final point of owning up to your own misunderstandings. You might think, "But I haven't misunderstood! And I haven't done anything wrong!" Well, you will need to let go of this idea a little if you hope to come to a harmonious resolution. The good news is that if you can do this, you may be surprised by just how ready other people are to follow suit, to drop grievances, and to find a happy way forward.

It might work to find not just points that you agree on, but goals that you both share. It may be that the only thing you agree on is that you would both like the argument to be resolved so you can get on with your respective lives. There is always a sense of cooperation when people feel as though they're striving toward the same thing—even if that thing is to be rid of one another!

A few tips to bear in mind:

- **Make people feel like they matter**. Just because you're having an argument, it doesn't mean that they're your enemy or that they're bad people. Make sure they know this! If appropriate, you can literally say, "I care about you," or, "this relationship matters to me."
- **Acknowledge and label emotions**, including your own. But it's important to do this without judgment or placing blame. Nobody feels how they feel *because* of anybody else.
- **Don't assume the worst in others**. Yes, there may have been an offense committed—but how big is it really? Was it intentional? Is it really something that can't be managed? When you scale down the size of the problem, it's easier to deal with.
- **Convey an attitude of cooperation** no matter what. Validate the other person by saying things like, "I can see where you're coming from," or, "That's a good point."
- If you must argue, **argue with the best version of the message** the other person is presenting—not the worst. The opposite of attacking a strawman is engaging respectfully with a "steel man." Take some time to reflect what the other person is saying, making their position look as good as possible. If they see that

you not only understand but sincerely respect their position, your disagreement with it will be far easier to accept.

- Understanding is different from agreeing. **Work hard to show you understand—even if you don't agree.** "It seems like you mean XYZ. Have I got that right?" This way, you are connecting and harmonizing, even as you recognize that you both have different perceptions, values, or goals.
- **Suspend your ego!** Don't preach, teach, or be condescending. Entertain the fact that you could be wrong—yes, even you! Say things like, "Oh, I didn't know that," and immediately admit when you've made a mistake. Not only will it inspire connection and resolution, it will make the other person far more willing to accept other claims you make more forcefully.
- **Normalize.** Conflict-averse people treat disagreement as a disaster—it's not. It's a normal part of life. In fact, it's an honor to face a worthy adversary or to come up against a worldview that challenges your own. So, thank the other person for disagreeing. Thank them for talking to you. Thank them for being honest. Just because you're having a conflict, it doesn't mean there's nothing of value

there or that you cannot value the other person and what they're bringing to that conflict. What determines the quality of a relationship is not the lack of conflict but the way in which that conflict is managed.

Technique 2: VOMP

VOMP is a simple four-step conflict-resolution technique that improves honesty and opens up communication in stressful relationships. The idea is to resolve small conflicts before they turn into big ones. The acronym stands for the following:

V – Voice or Vent

O – Own

M – Moccasins (stepping into someone else's shoes with empathy)

P – Plan

You start by **voicing or venting** your own feelings on the matter, whatever they are. Here is your chance to say your piece without interruption. Be careful to use only "I" statements that do not implicate or blame the other person, and be as honest as you can without veering into disrespect. And then—you guessed it—it's the other person's turn. In formal mediation, there is usually someone to make sure that each person is given a fair chance to vent/voice. In everyday conflict, you will need to have enough discipline to do this for yourself, even in the heat of the moment.

Then, each person **owns their part of the conflict**, accepting responsibility for what is rightly their contribution. What words, actions, and even attitudes have you each brought to the conflict to make it what it is? Crucially, this is not about weighing up who was more wrong or who the victim is, and it's not about blame. It's about gaining clarity on why the conflict is happening and mutually making a show of accepting one's role in that.

With **empathy** ("step into another person's moccasins"), you deliberately enter into their perspective and try to see things through their eyes. This is not a cognitive exercise but an emotional one. As we've seen already, we don't have to agree with, like, or even comprehend a person's unique experience to validate it and have empathy for it.

Finally, the plan part of the acronym is about **moving forward in a concrete way**. The best way to resolve any tension and dispute is to mutually agree on a path of action in the future. Where do you both now stand? What will change going forward? What happens next? You don't need to have a perfectly worked out strategy to fix all issues, but at least identify the very next step forward that you both agree on. You want to end a discussion with a shared feeling of having achieved something and worked together on creating a plan that serves you both.

Here's a brief example.

A: "You lent my camera and returned it damaged, and I'm really angry that it's broken because I need to use it now. I trusted you and I feel really irritated right now." (Vent/voice)

B: "I know, I know... but the camera was already damaged when you gave it to me. I would never break something of yours and then lie about it."

A: "Okay, fine, I believe you. I guess I just lost my temper because it seemed like you were trying to say the camera wasn't broken, or that it wasn't your fault." (Owning their part)

B: "Well, I am saying that it *wasn't* my fault. But I think the way I worded it was probably a bit too rude. I really am sorry that it's broken; I know how much you love that camera." (Owning their part, plus some empathy)

A: "No, it's understandable that you were rude—I was accusing you of something you didn't do. I would have responded the same way!" (Returning empathy)

B: "Look, I have a friend who does repairs on this kind of thing. Shall I ask him for his opinion?"

A: "Yeah, thanks, that might be helpful."

Technique 3: Nonviolent Communication

Unless we're in the habit of punching people who disagree with us, most of us wouldn't consider the way we communicate to be "violent." But according to Marshall Rosenberg, an expert mediator, author, and originator of the nonviolent communication framework (NVP), we may be doing just that when we are forceful, coercive, manipulative, judgmental, passive aggressive, or controlling.

NVP is a much loved and useful model for all kinds of conflicts and disputes—provided the parties involved are committed to using the framework in good faith. In fact, Rosenberg's techniques have been used for everything from divorce mediation and marriage counseling to supporting peace talks in the Middle East. The process is not so much a technique as an entire paradigm. The four simple stages/steps are as follows:

Observation

You begin with impartial observation. We note what is actually factually true with the impartiality of a neutral third-person observer. Instead of saying, "You don't value my opinion," you say, "I notice that you frequently interrupt me when I'm talking." When we make observations, there are no judgments or interpretations. We are just finding an agreed upon foundation on which to build. This cannot be done if you are leading with accusations, distortions, and defensiveness.

Feelings

You then share your feelings on the above observed facts. Truthfully, it can be quite difficult to tell the difference sometimes! Again, these are emotions that you own. They're yours, so you describe them that way. "I feel sad," instead of, "You're making me so depressed." Of course, we are all interconnected and constantly influence one another, but we do not seek the source or cause of emotions (i.e., other people). We just state what they are.

If you fail to take ownership and honestly express your emotions, the other person is likely to take it personally (and suddenly, it's not about you anymore!) or fight back and argue. If you share your emotions neutrally, however, the other person can respond to that, or else do the same and share their emotions in the same way.

Needs

According to Rosenberg, people communicate primarily to get their needs met. That's the underlying purpose of all communication. Once you've located yourself in the context of the conflict, made observations, and shared how you feel, you can express what all this means to you and what exactly you're trying to achieve. Everybody has needs, and every human shares the same basic *human* needs: to be heard, to be able to contribute, to be respected, to be valued, to belong, etc.

There are of course different types of needs and different ways to express them. "I need you to stop sending me documents in the wrong format" is a very specific need, whereas "I need you to consider my position before you act" is a far more universal one. We also need to take care how we frame our needs, again not implicating other people. Consider the previous two needs—both were expressed as something the other person needs to do. Rosenberg would say that this is in fact violent. Instead, we should express our needs without coercion, blame, or obligation.

"I need to receive correctly formatted documents."

"I have a need to be considered and respected."

See the difference?

Requests

Only once the previous three bases have been covered is it a good idea to move on to requests of others. Too many people have conversations that *begin* with demands and expectations. This seldom works. Rather, let the request come naturally from you expressing your need.

"I have a need to receive correctly formatted documents. This lets me do my job more quickly and easily. Can I ask that you only send me documents that fit the specifications I've given you?"

While the previous steps are about observation, listening, and expressing, this step is about making a direct request for change or action on someone else's part. Requests have the best chance of being met when they are expressed as naturally connected to observations, emotions, and needs; when they're reasonable and realistic; and when they're presented as a request and not a demand.

The most important thing here is that requests are just that—requests. The other person is never obliged to comply. Even if you have a universal need ("I need to not be abused or mistreated"), that doesn't strictly entitle you to force this behavior from someone else. You might be wondering, then, what happens if someone refuses your request. Well, each of us is always at liberty to terminate a relationship. We cannot decide what other people's actions are. But we can decide our own, and we can make conscious choices to identify our needs and determine how we are going to get them met.

If we are with someone who continues to abuse us, we can communicate our need and request that they meet it. But if they don't, then the onus is on us to extract ourselves from that relationship. In this way, we increase our connection and interdependence on other people while *simultaneously* taking responsibility for meeting our own needs.

Communicating with Difficult People

Sooner or later, despite your very best efforts, you will encounter someone who refuses to communicate or come to a resolution. Most people find themselves in conflict because they're hurt, confused, or defensive—but this can be worked through. On the other hand, if someone is not willing to meet you halfway or find common ground, then a different approach becomes necessary.

Being assertive does not mean being rude or confrontational. It simply means standing strong in what you believe and defending what is important. We can all become better communicators by dropping our ego, being more open and receptive, and welcoming a bit of vulnerability. BUT there are certainly circumstances when you need to do the opposite—firm up, enforce a boundary, and stand strong.

If we use NVC, we are able to honestly express our feelings and needs without encroaching on the needs and rights of others. But what about when they encroach on us? Here are two quick techniques to protect yourself and stand your ground while *still* respecting the other person.

- **Fogging**. When dealing with an upset and noncooperative person, it doesn't make sense to try to engage. So don't. Fogging means calmly going along with aggressive people so as not to further encourage any defensiveness or argument. In effect, you are making yourself a smooth, gray, boring surface onto which nothing sticks! That way, the strong feeling has to pass eventually. In the meantime, you haven't upset yourself or prolonged the conflict.
- **The broken record technique**. If you're stating a boundary or saying no and someone keeps pushing at that, it's a good idea to plainly and simply keep repeating your no/boundary again and again without adding any further information onto which they can "hook." Be polite, be calm, but don't budge. Be a broken record that gives precisely the

same answer each time. It's a way to be firm without being rude.

Both fogging and the broken record technique can be used together.

"Please lend me that money. I'll pay you back, honest."

"I'm sorry, no, I can't."

"But why not? I don't see what the big deal is. You're making it seem like I'm asking you for a kidney."

"Uh huh."

"So will you give it to me?"

"No, sorry. I can't lend you the money."

"I can't believe this. You're being so rude."

"Mm."

"You've always been stingy like this. I bet you love lauding it over me. Well, I don't need it, not from you, anyway!"

"Okay."

"Typical! And it's not even that much I'm asking for. So what do you say, come on, please?"

"I can't give you the money, sorry."

As you can see in the above exchange, one person is valiantly trying to coerce, pressure, and guilt the other into doing what they want, but the person is holding strong—without being rude. By combining neutral and even bland responses ("uh huh, okay") with the broken record message of saying no, eventually the other person runs out of steam and gives up.

The trick here is to constantly maintain a **calm, composed demeanor that is non-reactive**. If you lose your temper or get hooked into arguing over details, the conversation will only escalate. Don't take any bait. Naturally, as soon as you can, remove yourself as far as possible from people who push boundaries this way!

The Six-Step Apology

Of course, it's always possible that you could be the one who is the main cause of the conflict! We'll end this chapter on what just might be one of the hardest communication skills to master—the art of apology. If you truly listen and are open and respectful, you will find that conflict of all kinds diminishes in your life. But none of us are perfect, and sometimes we will find ourselves needing to smooth over ruffled feathers, accept our culpability, and make a clear show of our remorse and our willingness to put things right.

According to Roy Lewicki, a professor emeritus of management and human resources at the Fisher College of Business at Ohio State University, there is a six-point narrative framework that every excellent apology ought to follow. Lewicki is a renowned authority on the art of negotiating and spent years studying what constitutes a good apology. He came to the realization that, like any other good story, an apology needs to hit all the right notes and follow the right structure.

Lewicki's suggestion is to **apologize as early as possible, do it sincerely, and do it without being forced**. Let's say you are Sister B in the example we covered earlier. You deliberately asked Sister A to juggle her schedule to squeeze in a meeting with you, and then dropped her when you realized that you yourself were double-booked. There's no getting around it—you messed up. Now how do you apologize so that it truly restores harmony again?

First of all, a few things *not* to do:

- Don't rush as though you were only interested in having the other person absolve you of wrong-doing and move on, pretending like nothing ever happened.
- Don't give a faux apology along the lines of "sorry you felt offended."

- Don't get angry or upset—it's not about you!

Step 1: Express genuine regret

It sounds obvious, but you have to begin at the beginning and say that you're sorry. Not passively sorry that the thing happened, but sorry for what you did. "I'm sorry I asked you to make plans to meet me and then dropped at the last minute."

Your tone makes all the difference. Don't be stroppy, insincere, annoyed, or sarcastic. Literally use the words "I'm sorry" and say them as early as possible.

Step 2: Explain what went wrong and why

This is your chance to explain what happened, letting the other person know that there was in fact a reason that you made the mistake you did. When we've been wronged, it's easy to get angry because we imagine that the other person did what they did simply because they didn't care, or even because they blatantly meant to hurt us. So begin by making it clear that this isn't the case.

Be careful, though; you don't want to give the impression that you're making excuses or not accepting responsibility. You just want to provide some context to let the person understand a little more about what went wrong. According to Lewicki,

> "It's trying to help the other party understand how this happened in a way where they can understand that it was a mistake or an error. It's an effort to put them in your shoes to get a sense of how and why it happened."

In our example, you could say, "What happened is that I accidentally double booked something else that weekend without realizing."

Step 3: Acknowledge your responsibility

This one can be a big stumbling block, but if you can do this genuinely, you will go a long way to lowering the defensiveness of the other person and will come across more sincerely. You need to own your actions. Don't accept that you did something and immediately follow it with "but" or an excuse. Just accept that you did it. Don't shift blame—especially not onto the person you wronged!—but at the same time, it's not necessary to beat yourself up. It sounds cheesy, but it can be therapeutic for someone to hear another person say, "I was wrong. I accept responsibility for that."

Be crystal clear about the role you played. Try not to make it seem like your actions were just a silly misunderstanding or an accident that isn't really your fault. For example, "It's my fault; I didn't pay attention to what I had written on my calendar, and I take responsibility for that."

Step 4: Repent!

Sounds dramatic, but if a person is sincerely apologetic, their apology needs to contain a declaration for repentance. This means you need to show a believable and genuine level of remorse. The best way to do this is to offer your assurance that it will never happen again—and mean it. Think about the last time you made a complaint as a customer. It's likely that endless platitudes only made you angrier—what you really wanted to hear was that the company truly was sorry for what they had done and regretted it. While it's not likely that many companies genuinely repent, you can be sure that *you* do when you give an apology.

"I wish I'd handled this whole scheduling thing better. I can't go back and change the past, but I can promise you that this will not happen again." Naturally, you really do need to keep this promise going forward.

Step 5: Make an offer of reparations

Saying you're sorry is a wonderful thing, but often, it's difficult to move forward because your actions have created a real inconvenience or even damage. You need to plainly acknowledge this and make a real gesture toward putting things right. This can be tricky sometimes because you cannot go back and undo the past. But what you can do is demonstrate to the other person that you have given things some thought and have come up with a realistic plan for what you can do in the future.

"I've set things up on a new calendar app so I don't get muddled again. I've also made sure to completely clear the next two weekends so we can get together soon—if you're available, that is."

"If there were actual damages, you can offer to pay for or repair the damages, or if there were [emotional] damages, then a dozen roses or a box of chocolates might do the work. I'm serious about that. Token offers of repentance that are above and beyond just the words are quite often quite symbolic," says Lewicki.

Step 6: Request forgiveness

Lewicki's research showed him something interesting: This aspect of the apology process was actually the least important. And yet, many people start with this part and immediately request to be forgiven . . . before they've even properly apologized. If you've covered each of the previous five steps as thoroughly as possible, though, then asking for forgiveness will seem like a natural progression and no big deal.

It can be simple: "Can you forgive me?" Remember to phrase this as a request—not a demand. If you come across as being entitled to forgiveness just because you've presented a nice apology, the other person will sense this, and you could undo all your hard work and end up with hurt feelings again.

You might be wondering—what happens if the other person doesn't accept your apology? There is only one thing to do: accept that. Remember that nobody is ever required to accept your apology or to forgive. Nobody likes to feel that they are the bad guy or that someone is still unhappy with them, but that is an unfortunate possibility if we've done them wrong—especially if the transgression is a pretty big one.

In that case, one of the most respectful things you can do is to honor that person's unhappiness and don't try to badger them into forgiving you. Especially don't try to rush them or make them feel bad for not immediately accepting your apology. Again, it's not about you. Even if they do accept your apology, try not to barge ahead and act as though nothing happened. An apology is a gesture offered in good will, and so is forgiving someone. Treasure that forgiveness and don't take it for granted or act entitled to it.

Handled correctly, a mistake followed by a sincere apology can actually strengthen a relationship and create more feelings of trust and connection. By the same token, a bad apology is a missed opportunity and, in some cases, can be perceived as even worse than the original offense.

Let's put it all together.

Here are a few badly constructed apologies:

"I feel so, so bad for smashing your car. I've been up all night and I feel just sick about it. Of course I'll pay for everything, but I want you to know it wasn't my fault. That guy just came out of nowhere. I'm still shaken up by it."—*While this apology has a definite offer to make things right, there isn't much else. The lack of repentance, regret, or responsibility, and the continued focus on bad **they** feel (i.e., not on how bad you feel for having a smashed car!) makes the apology ring hollow.*

"Of course I'm sorry we've had this little misunderstanding. I've already said that. We can't do anything about it now, though, and what's done is done. Can you just move past it already?"—*This apology is likely to cause more offense. It contains none of the elements except a request—demand, even—for forgiveness. It also minimizes the event ("misunderstanding") and frames the offense as something passive and completely out of their control, implying that the person who is offended is really to blame. A great way to start a fight!*

"Oh my God, I am so sorry! I've been such a moron. It was one hundred percent my fault. I don't know how it happened. I can't believe it. I'm sorry, truly. I wish I hadn't even gotten into your car; none of this would have happened. Oh my God!"—*This apology comes from a genuine place of regret and remorse . . . but that's not really enough. Over-the-top expressions of remorse need to lead to a sense that something will change in the future. There needs to be a feeling that all this remorse and regret will have a positive outcome somehow.*

Let's end with a quick look at a model apology, according to Lewicki.

"I am so truly sorry about what happened. It was a stupid mistake that I regret; I just lost control of the vehicle. I accept total responsibility for everything, and I know I should have done better. If I could go back and do things differently, I would in a heartbeat, but I can't. What I can do, though, is offer to pay for any and all damage. Please let me know if there's anything else I can do to make it right. I hope that in time, you can forgive me."

Note that a really good apology doesn't have to be long or overwrought. It just needs to cover all six bases and be sincere. That's it.

Summary:

- The goal during conflict is to increase positive feelings for everyone involved. One way to do this is with Carroll's COIN framework—context, observations, impact, and next (follow-up actions). Use plenty of "I" statements, pause often, and be as clear and direct as possible. When giving feedback, focus on what can be done in the future rather than what has already been done.
- There are many ways to navigate communication when you disagree. The agreement frame helps the other person release their resistance to your perspective because you are able to really support *their* views or values first and seek common ground that puts you on the same team.
- The art of saying no includes understanding the different kinds of assertions, including basic assertions (statements of facts and limits), empathic assertions (asserting needs and limits whilst acknowledging others' with kindness), consequence assertions (following through with consequences of not respecting your boundary), discrepancy assertions (drawing attention to difference between what was agreed and what is happening), and negative feeling assertions (owning your own emotions and stating them).
- VOMP is another technique and stands for voice/vent, own, moccasins, and plan. Say

your piece and allow the other person to say theirs, own your part in the conflict, show empathy for their perspective, and then move forward with a concrete plan on how to act in the future.
- Marshall Rosenberg's nonviolent communication is about making neutral observations, expressing feelings with "I" statements, sharing needs, and making reasonable and respectful requests.
- If none of these three techniques work, you can manage a difficult person by "fogging" (being as neutral and non-reactive as possible) or repeating boundaries like a "broken record" until they lose interest.
- Finally, learn the six elements of a successful and genuine apology: express regret and remorse, explain yourself, accept full responsibility, repent, make an offer for reparations, and, only at the end, request forgiveness. Realize that you are not entitled to forgiveness, and accept whatever happens with grace.

Chapter 5. Goal-Oriented Communication

How to Persuade Anyone

So far, we've focused on listening, validation, and ways to resolve conflict and misunderstanding. These are without a doubt the heavy lifters when it comes to learning to communicate better, cultivate a sense of charisma and charm, and deepen interpersonal connections of all kinds. But in certain contexts (for example, in business or in education), you don't just want to master receiving a message. You want to create your own message . . . and make sure that it lands on its audience with the most influence and impact possible. In other words, there are times when you will want to persuade someone.

To put it very simply, **persuasion is trying to change someone's mind**. A big part of being a masterful communicator is learning to genuinely receive, read, and understand other people and get inside their perspectives. In this final chapter, we'll be looking at *our* perspectives—and exactly how we can communicate them so that others adopt them for themselves. All communication has a purpose. And at some point, that purpose will be to actively influence our audience—whether that's a single person reading our email, a team of our peers, or a hall filled with thousands of people.

The golden rule in persuasive communication is, surprise, surprise, to **know your audience**. Luckily, in learning the previous chapter's skills of listening, validating, reading body language, etc., we have already gone some way to doing this. Before we continue, it's worth saying that persuasive communication does *not* mean manipulation. It means the artful and deliberate use of language to convey our meaning in a way that best achieves our purpose.

It's an art that traces back to Aristotle, and arguably back even further, to the very dawn of human communication (we might even guess that the primary reason for communication evolving in the first place was as a tool by which to influence and affect one another!). Almost two thousand years ago, Aristotle expounded on what he saw as the four primary strategies to reach and influence an audience. In his treatise *Rhetoric* during the fourth century BCE, he elevated persuasion to an art form. In Aristotle's time, oration was an honored art and tradition, and all educated men were expected to know how to correctly tailor their approach when addressing a group.

Four Modes of Persuasion

1. Ethos

The first mode of persuasion is called an appeal to ethos, i.e., **an address that rests on credibility to persuade**. What do we mean by credibility? Any time we trust and revere a professional or expert opinion, we do so because that opinion carries a certain credibility. We find it believable. We are persuaded by mastery and knowledge, which we assume belong to people who are in the know or who possess the right or the experience to speak on a certain topic.

It's not just about qualifications or titles, however. A mother of nine's perspective on childbirth will tend to have more credibility than a random man's; however, that man, if he is, for example, a world-renowned obstetrician, may have as much or more credibility—on certain aspects of childbirth, at least. Ethos is a question of reputation, authority, and trustworthiness. It's about the social standing and knowledge of the person speaking rather than just the words they're saying.

Marketers use this mode of persuasion when they dress an actor in a white lab coat and make him stand in front of a board covered with scientific-looking diagrams and charts in order to sell you toothpaste. A motivational speaker may successfully use an appeal to authority in the same way, showcasing certain clothing, styles, postures, ways of speaking, and attitudes that convey their authority to speak on their topic.

Indeed, many gurus and cult leaders have so mastered an appeal to ethos that whatever they say is perceived with reverence and credibility simply because of the way they've presented that appeal and how they've positioned themselves as experts (whether they are or not!).

Examples of ethos:

- A doctor promoting a certain brand of cigarette in an ad.
- A well-connected older celebrity talking about the problems in the film industry.
- An older and wiser mentor giving you advice in your career.

2. Pathos

An appeal to pathos is entirely different. **Pathos is about emotional persuasion**, and considering how easy it is for emotion to override duty or logic, this mode can be very powerful, indeed. But it's perhaps because of how easy it is to use that this form of persuasion is usually less respected than other forms. Think about a cheesy advert for an animal charity that obviously and blatantly pulls on your heartstrings. The audience may feel sorry about the images of sad puppies and kittens, but they're also keenly aware of the emotional manipulation, which means that the tactic could just as easily backfire.

But when pathos is used well, it works well. It requires that the speaker has a deep and sophisticated understanding of who their audience actually is, what their desires are, and what their deepest needs could be. Then, they speak to that. If the audience is known to value, for example, freedom and independence, then the argument is framed in these terms. The speaker might choose to frame their argument or narrative in terms that speak to these values, driving home the point that all free-thinking and autonomous individuals can't help but come to the very same conclusion they have (of course, if your audience is also intelligent, they may sniff out the irony in this!).

On the other hand, you might want to speak to your audience's emotion so that you can counter it. For example, an inspiring speaker may keenly understand the fear and uncertainty the audience may be feeling, but choose words that counteract that unwanted emotion and inspire another emotion—in this case, let's say courage and decisiveness. The speaker will be really successful at inducing this state of courageousness if she understands the emotional position her audience is starting out at.

When you use pathos, you are not constructing an argument or making a point based on logic, facts, or morals. You are appealing solely to the way people feel. If a lawyer wants the jury not to vote against his client, he will try to cultivate feelings of pity, compassion, and forgiveness. Or if the lawyer for the other side wants to achieve the opposite, he will try to speak to feelings of anger and injustice in the jury.

Examples of pathos:

- A picture of a crying refugee child in an activist campaign, with an appeal for donations beneath it.
- Someone getting their way by playing cute or being sexy.
- A YouTube thumbnail with bold yellow letters: THEY'RE LYING TO YOU.

3. Logos

Finally, the appeal to logos is an appeal to logic or rationality—or, and this is important, the *appearance* of logic and rationality. An argument presented with research to back it up, and a logical, internally consistent argument to make its point, is making an appeal to logos. Any time you bring up proof, evidence, reasoning, facts and figures, or even common sense, you are appealing to logos.

One broad type of argument you can make is one that rests on deductive reasoning. This is essentially the scientific method: You start out with a tentative theory to explain something, this inspires a hypothesis, you do an experiment or make observations, and depending on what you find, you come to conclusions. You begin with the broad and general and deduce the specific (incidentally, this is *not* the form of reasoning most used by Sherlock Holmes!). A simple example of deductive reasoning is:

All Greeks are philosophers (premise 1).
Aristotle is Greek (premise 2).
Therefore, Aristotle is a philosopher (conclusion).

As you can see, deductive reasoning is about the *form* of the argument, not the content. The above argument is valid (i.e., it follows logically in structure), but it isn't *sound* since the premises are not true. For an argument to be sound, both the premises and the conclusion need to be true. An argument can be valid, however, without either premises or conclusion being true.

Inductive reasoning goes the other direction, i.e., it uses specific observations to move to a more general theory or principle. For example, "every Greek person I've met so far has been a philosopher; therefore, this person I've just met, who is Greek, is probably also a philosopher." Of course, the quality of the conclusion in an inductive argument rests on the quality of the observations. If you've only ever met two Greeks in your life, for example, your conclusion is quite a weak one!

You can recognize an appeal to logic by reference to science, to rationality, or to facts and figures (or, again, the *appearance* of such things).

Examples of logos:

- A government-funded pamphlet says, "One out of every five students reports being bullied at school."
- A doctor releases a paper on sulfites in the diet, and it's published in a journal.

- A woman wearing a pantsuit and a lanyard asks people in a hotel lobby to move somewhere else. They do.

4. Kairos

Kairos is the fourth of Aristotle's modes, and one that might be a little harder to understand from a modern perspective. Kairos can be broadly translated to mean *opportunity* or *right time* in Greek. This is an appeal that rests heavily on when it's made, i.e., it's about identifying the perfect moment to launch the message. Sometimes, your audience is most receptive after a particular event or realization—if you present your case then, it has the best chance of being received. For example, politicians often wait for some negative event to pounce with a pre-prepared message that the public will be far more willing to accept than if it had been proposed at any other time. Likewise, you might wait for a friend to be in a calm, relaxed state of mind before broaching a delicate topic with them.

Kairos is about appropriateness. It's about being aware of who your audience is, where and when you're addressing them, and in what context. How are people currently feeling? What came before? What is the environment, and how does this impact the degree to which people can hear and understand you?

Examples of kairos:

- Advertising wrinkle cream to people in the weeks leading up to their birthdays.
- Going to console your crush right after they've broken up with their current partner.
- Addressing a room full of parents, you start your speech with a sweet joke about your four-year-old nephew.

Using the Four Modes of Persuasion

It's not that any of the four modes is better or more effective than any other. It's more a question of knowing your audience and knowing exactly which mode will work best for them. That's important—**it's not about which mode fits *you* best or fits your message best. It's about putting your message in a form that your audience is most likely to hear and register**. The skill of a great and persuasive orator, then, is not about how well they can communicate, but how well they can communicate **to** their chosen audience.

Let's consider an example. Let's say in your workplace, you're trying to make a case for using some newly available funds to get everyone signed up for a training course. Since others have their own ideas for what to do with this money, you need to actively persuade people round to your point of view. How?

You might have a word with your immediate supervisor first. Knowing a little about them, you guess that an argument to emotion would work best. You ask, what do they need currently and what is their most pressing emotion? Realizing that they have been irritated for a long time about picking up the slack of less-qualified staff, you tailor your argument to appease this sense. "If we all completed this training, it would not only boost morale and build up team cohesion, it would also empower everyone with some new skills so we're better able to cope."

You might not blatantly say, "And that will lead to less work for you," but you are speaking to their emotion (irritation) and arguing in a way that they will likely hear and resonate with. You would dwell on the positive emotional benefits of your plan ("Just think! No more having to fix up other people's mistakes!") and present your argument as a solution to their pains.

However, if you were speaking to a fellow colleague who already felt overburdened and might not be interested in taking on a new training program, you might decide to appeal to authority instead. Crucially, you have to think of *who* your colleague actually considers an authority! You decide to frame your argument as personal development and mention that their favorite self-help guru recommends ongoing career development as a question of self-respect and autonomy.

Later on, when you have a chance to address the entire office, which constitutes a mixed group, you lean more heavily on an appeal to time, place, and appropriateness (Kairos) and present a more generally appealing argument that will speak to everyone more broadly. Being keenly aware of your workplace's culture, you deliver an argument you know is in keeping with the overall tone, mood, and style.

It's likely in life that you'll have to make a compelling argument that includes elements of all these persuasive modes. In that case, here are a few tips:

- To establish your credibility (ethos), **lead with your genuine credentials**, experience, and expertise—and don't oversell them! If you cannot establish credibility yourself, refer to someone else who does have that authority.
- The best and most authentic way to appeal to pathos is to **share your heartfelt and honest personal experiences**. If they're unique to you and yet somehow speak to universal themes, all the better. Be mindful of not

appearing emotionally manipulative, however, and try to steer clear of inciting guilt or fear in others.
- Another way to appeal to pathos is to **be vulnerable**. Share a secret, open up, and "go first" emotionally speaking—it will create a sense of trust and shared humanity.
- Pathos can also be addressed by using **vivid metaphors** and colorful, even poetic language. If you're impassioned about something, share it. Let your raw enthusiasm and energy shine through.
- If your argument needs a little more logos, don't underestimate the power of some **hard data**. Statistics, graphics, and concrete values—money can be especially effective!—can make the point quickly and neutrally.
- Whatever mode you're using, begin any message by capturing attention. Then, consider closely what your audience's **need** is, and speak to that. Start with the problem, outline your argument, and then paint a vision of the future where they behave or believe as you'd like them to, i.e., their problem has been solved. Your argument is essentially a demonstration of why your idea is in fact a way for them to get *their* needs met.

The Office.

Our final chapter focuses on a very specific form of communication—communication in professional contexts and with colleagues and employers. It's not that the skills we've already explored do not apply—they do—it's rather that the workplace requires additional rules of etiquette and formality that take extra consideration.

At work, good communication is not just something nice to have so that people get along. Communication is non-negotiable. No matter what your role is or what work you're doing, doing that work will depend at some point on how well you can share your own message and hear the messages of others. **All the same considerations apply when thinking about verbal and nonverbal communication, but in the workplace, we have to consider the enormous role that both written and electronic communication plays, too.**

Workplace Communication Etiquette

Etiquette sounds like a horribly old-fashioned word, but the truth is as social beings, we are always following some form of etiquette whether we're aware of it or not. A simple dictionary definition says that etiquette is "the customary code of polite behavior in society or among members of a particular profession or group."

When talking to friends, family, or romantic partners, customary codes and politeness are still important, but it's in the workplace where communication is really stripped down to its most formal, impersonal, and rule bound. Therefore, what makes you a good communicator at home or with friends will not necessarily make you a good communicator at work!

When thinking about workplace communication, there are three things to consider:

- The GOAL of communication
- The CONTENT of our communication
- The WAY we communicate that content, also known as the MEDIUM

If you can correctly identify each of these three, you can more consciously communicate your message and hear other people's. If you're in a new workplace or are trying to deal with potential conflict or misunderstanding, it's worth slowing everything down and being very deliberate in the way you approach your communication—i.e., don't expect to automatically know how to do the right thing.

Step 1: Let your goal decide your medium

It sounds unbelievable, but many people launch into an attempt at communication without actually knowing what they're trying to achieve or why. They may correctly perceive that there's a misunderstanding, or know that some kind of connection needs to be made, but things are not defined any more clearly than that.

Have you ever received a rambling email filled with all sorts of miscellany from a colleague and reached the end of it thinking, "Well, what was the point of all *that*?" You were probably on the receiving end of someone who had not clarified their purpose and goal before attempting to communicate! Nevertheless, their lack of clarity doesn't have to become your lack of clarity.

You need to understand your reason for communicating. Let's say, for example, that you are requesting that a completed report be revisited since there are serious errors that now make the report unusable. You think you should get in touch with the team who drafted the report, but first, you pause and think—what exactly are you trying to achieve? By asking that question, you take those actions (and only those actions) that will help you achieve that goal, and cut down on the possibility of rambling, confusion, or misunderstanding. You decide that your goal is to draw attention to the errors and to thank the team but politely request that they recompile it by a certain date so that you can use it as planned.

Once you've identified this goal, you can allow it to inform your choice of medium, i.e., via which channel you're going to communicate through. In this case, you decide that a properly written email sent to all members of the team will do the job. If your goal was simply to keep someone updated about a deadline or answer a quick question, a text message might have worked, as could literally popping your head into their office and telling them in passing. A more serious topic may warrant meeting in person with enough time to prepare beforehand.

Here are a few more questions that may help you fine-tune the kind of message you're going to send:

- Is there any urgency, or is the issue time sensitive in any way?
- Will the information be sensitive or confidential?
- How many people need to receive this message?
- Do you require a response to this message or not? If so, what kind?
- Is your goal with this communication more general or more specific?
- What is the relationship between you and the receiver—are they hierarchically higher or lower than you, or are they a peer? What exactly is the nature of your

role regarding them, and what is the context of that relationship?

In answering these questions and giving it some thought, you decide that you need to act quickly if you want to get your report redone. The information needs to go to five people in particular, but not to anyone else, as the material is confidential. You want to communicate very specific changes you wish to make, and need to know that they've received and understood these details and that they can comply within the time frame. As you can see, you already have the framework of an effective message coming together...

Step 2: Factor in your company's unique communication culture

You've identified the goal and the medium, but there may still be very specific ways of doing things that are unique to your company. Etiquette rules are general and exist to ease interactions, but you will also need to carefully consider your audience and the special rules they follow beyond normal etiquette.

If you work in a relaxed setting where management makes a point of not interfering with people's work–life balance, it's probably a bad idea to send a demanding email at 1 a.m. on Sunday morning. Likewise, if management tends to maintain a very formal, structured work atmosphere, then you will need to be mindful of following protocols about copying in the right people in emails or keeping the correct records and minutes of meetings no matter how small or brief.

Here, an eye to the kind of rhetoric you're using—pathos, ethos, or logos—will be useful, too. Don't assume that there is no place for pathos in formal workplaces. Any appeal to company loyalty, striving for excellence, or maintaining high standards as a point of pride is, in fact, an appeal to the emotions. Likewise, don't assume that logos or ethos are always appropriate. Company culture might be such that you are expected to make your own claims rather than appeal to the authority of some third party or to focus on practical implementation rather than making a more academic presentation of the facts and figures, as you would with logos.

Perhaps the most crucial considering will be kairos, or appropriateness. Think carefully about when you will put forward your message, and in what context. It may seem insignificant, but the time of year, month, day, or even minute can influence how well your message is received. The medium may also need to change depending on the best time of delivery—for example, you may wish to forego an email and wait until you can speak in person.

In our example, if you imagine that you're in a medium-sized but relatively relaxed work environment, you might send a properly worded but not overly formal email. Knowing your company's business, you understand that people value directness, honesty, and sincerity. And knowing the five people on the team, you approach the message simply and clearly, highlighting the mistake but in a friendly and nonconfrontational way and politely asking for their help rather than demanding or formally requesting their compliance.

Step 3: Watch your tone

This is the step where we take into account all the ordinary rules of communication we've already explored. Is your tone too aggressive or passive aggressive? Are there any assumptions, premature judgments, or inflexible attitudes that are getting in the way of meeting the goal? Ironically, in professional communication, it is more important than ever to be emotionally aware and able to manage and harness emotions rather than letting them dominate or derail.

In our example, you need to be aware of the fact that the people who've compiled the report may react defensively if they feel they're being attacked or unfairly criticized. You may also notice your own feelings of awkwardness, annoyance, or guilt. None of these are a problem, however, if they're properly acknowledged, harnessed, and managed. For example, you could bring awareness to this emotional reality, but control it and steer it to your own ends:

"I realize this is a little awkward, and I wasn't entirely sure how to broach the topic with you, but the references section on this report will need to be redone entirely. The rest of the report was extremely helpful. In addition, I'm glad that we caught this error now, and the report has definitely given us the opportunity to slow down and rethink a few faulty assumptions we've been making."

It is a myth that professional workplace communication needs to be emotion-free. Emotion has a place in every area of human life and always will. It's just that in the workplace, we are more deliberate about how that emotion plays out in the way we meet our goals. The above response acknowledges emotions without making them the sole determiner of behavior.

Still, plenty of conflicts occur purely based on misunderstandings of tone. If you're unsure about how your email is coming across, get a colleague to read it and give you feedback. No matter the message, goal, or context, favor clarity and simplicity. The following checklist can help you stay on track:

- Is your message respectful? You don't have to agree, but are you conveying basic tact and courtesy to the other person's perspective?
- Is your message focused exclusively on meeting your goal? Have you avoided expressing negativity without suggesting any solution?
- Is your message professionally neutral, i.e., have you removed any personal opinions that could be divisive, offensive, or awkward?
- Have you taken care with the formatting details? This means proofreading text, enunciating clearly when you speak, and learning the appropriate titles for people or the right way to pronounce certain terms.

The Seven Cs of Effective Workplace Communication

Granted, you will not always have the opportunity to sit and carefully pre-plan all your communication. Still, over time, with constant awareness of why you are communicating, what you are communicating, and how (not to mention to whom), you will gradually start to appreciate communication as a brilliant tool you can use to further your own ends.

The "seven Cs" are a useful set of principles that you can use to guide you as you improve your workplace communication skills. No, this doesn't mean you will never be misunderstood or that people will always be cooperative (that's *their* part of the communication process, right?), but it does make it far, far more likely.

Clarity

Before you can hope to have the other person understand what you're saying, *you* need to have that clarity for yourself. Make sure to confirm that the other person has received the message by asking clarifying questions, or even get them to paraphrase what they've heard you say. At the end of communication, both of you should feel that there are no uncertainties in the message that has been shared from either side.

- Use simple language. Being formal and professional doesn't mean you have to use clunky, vague vocabulary! Say "use" instead of "utilize." Business jargon can be not only annoying but also can muddy your meaning. Don't say "close of play," for example, when what you really mean is "5 p.m. today."

- While idioms and metaphors can help with more emotion-centered language, avoid it when you're trying to be clear.
- It might be helpful to literally put your goal out there. "I'd like to get the complete and updated report done by 5 p.m. today."

Conciseness

Getting your point across without any unnecessary fluff. Softening, hedging language (*you know, sort of, if you know what I mean, maybe, kind of* . . .) can not only come across as unconfident and incompetent, it can also confuse your message. The more you say, the more there is to misunderstand. Go back over your message and see if you can extract the essence and get rid of the rest.

Concrete

This means to be backed up by facts, or else real, solid, actual, and specific. Basically, don't be vague. It's better to say "the first five references were done incorrectly" than "the report could have used a little more polish . . ."

Correct

This refers both to the rules of language (grammar, spelling, syntax) but also to the "rules" of whatever format you're using. This is especially important if you're making an appeal to logos or want to convey a sense of your own authority and trustworthiness. Small inaccuracies can distract at best, and completely undermine the message at worst. So, in our example, double and triple check that you are in fact correct about the errors you've found in the report!

Consideration

You know what your goal is, but what is theirs? Politeness is a minimum, but apply all the same skills of listening and validation we've already covered to acknowledge and respect the other person's perspective. What is their communication style, what are they struggling with, and how can you make them feel heard and seen while at the same time getting them to understand you?

Completeness

This is the truth, the whole truth, and nothing but the truth! You want to leave every conversation feeling as though what needed to be said has fully been said. An important detail is to make sure that you're ending by identifying next steps. What do you expect the other person to do? What will you do? Does everybody know what to expect of the other party, and how, and by when?

It's a good idea to end every interaction with a recap and a "call to action"—i.e., summarize what happens next.

Courtesy

There is never, ever a need to be rude, confrontational, or aggressive. Even in disagreement or misunderstanding, we can conduct ourselves with civility and respect—in fact, seeking to connect with others becomes *more* important as confusion or negative feelings arise, not *less*. Courtesy is just what empathy and compassion look like in a professional workplace.

In our example, courtesy is simply being polite enough to thank people for the report they've already compiled, finding a few words of positive feedback, and signing off the email with warmth and friendliness. It's very simple, really. Thank people for everything—their time, their attention, their contribution—say please when you can, and make space for people to respond without interruption, rushing, or judgment.

Summary:

- Persuasion is about trying to change or influence someone's mind, and it rests on knowing what that person's values, perspectives, and needs are so you can address them directly.
- According to Aristotle, the four main modes of persuasion are ethos (appeal to authority), pathos (appeal to emotion), logos (appeal to reason), and kairos (making an argument at the right time and place). Good oration and rhetoric are not about which mode fits you or your message best, but knowing how to put your message in a form that the audience is most likely to hear.
- To speak to pathos, be vulnerable or share a personal experience or even a secret. To speak to logos, use hard data and evidence or a deductive or inductive argument. To speak to ethos, share genuine and relevant credentials. In all cases, try to understand your audience's emotional state, their perspective, and their most pressing need, then present your message in terms that will appeal to them most.
- Workplace communication runs on all the same communication rules, but we have to consider the bigger role that written and electronic communication plays, too. Professional communication is more about appropriateness, politeness, custom, convention, and formality.

- We need to consider the goal, content, and medium to the message, as well as the audience. First, clarify the reason for communication and let that decide the most appropriate medium. Factor in your company's unique communication culture and be mindful of your tone.
- Professional communication should follow the seven Cs: It should be clear, concise, correct, concrete, considerate, complete, and courteous.

Summary Guide

CHAPTER 1. THE BASICS ARE NOT SO BASIC

- The best mindset to adopt in order to become a better communicator is the one that will best allow you to connect, meet your needs, solve problems, and express yourself.
- Begin by asking yourself what your default communication style is: aggressive, passive-aggressive, or manipulative. None of these styles actually achieves the ultimate goal of communication, however.
- The way you communicate is a choice. Assertive communication is the ability to express needs, wants, thoughts, and feelings directly without disrespecting or controlling others. Mature conversationalists are self-controlled, balanced, relaxed, open, and respectful.
- Communicating well is simple and easy, but we need to remove the formidable psychological barriers that stand in the way. With awareness, we can remove them and improve our communication skills.
- Barriers to good conversation include assumptions, strong negative emotions like anger and aggression (which inspire defensiveness), preconceived ideas and prejudice, fear, inflexibility and a need to

control, premature evaluation and judgment, and other negative conversational habits like interrupting or one-upping.
- Good conversation is firstly about the degree of concordance, harmony, and synchronicity between you and the person you're talking to, i.e., rapport.
- We can increase rapport by mirroring and matching both nonverbal and verbal expression. This can be done with internal and external cues, voice and language, content, and chunking style (i.e., up or down).
- When reading someone's body language, pay attention to microexpressions, their overall posture and orientation in space, as well as their degree of eye contact. Paralinguistics refers to information carried in the tone, pace, pitch, etc. of the voice.
- Think in terms of overall openness or closedness, but remember that no single detail is decisive and conclusive, and that observations should always be compared against a baseline.

CHAPTER 2. TOOLS OF THE CHARMING

- Having charm and charisma is not about you. It's about the other person and making them feel heard, liked, and supported.

- Dr. Albrecht explains that conversations contain three elements: declaratives, questions, and qualifiers. The rule of three tells us that we should not have three declarative statements in a row and should instead mix it up with a question or a qualifier.
- It's not really about the content of what you say but the emotional implications and the energy in *how* you say it.
- Conversational threading is a technique that will help you ensure you never run out of things to say. Listen to what the other person says, pick out a few noteworthy threads, then run with one of them. When the conversation dries up, return to these threads and pick up another one and follow that instead. Be patient, ask open-ended questions, and listen for emotions.
- Being a good everyday conversationalist is about being open-minded, spontaneous, and genuine. Keep things flowing!

CHAPTER 3. EQ > IQ

- There is no communication without emotions. That means that conversational intelligence is emotional intelligence. EQ is a mix of three skills: awareness of emotions, harnessing emotions, and managing emotions.

- If we are emotionally aware, we are able to identify what we are feeling in a conversation as well as observe and comprehend what another person is feeling—even if it's wildly different from our own experience. We are also then in a position to harness those emotions and to proactively and consciously choose a response.
- Slow down or pause, reflect what you're being told, and see if you can put the newly identified and named emotion to good use.
- Managing emotions means being conscious and deliberate: We can accept and acknowledge how we feel but still make conscious choices about our behavior according to our chosen goals.
- Validation is the process of genuinely hearing, seeing, and witnessing another person's lived reality and allowing it to be what it is. It's crucial in good communication. Validation is not agreement or reinforcement but recognizing emotions for what they are. It can be emotional, behavioral, or cognitive—or all three.
- Good listening is the ability to be open and receptive, to accept what we're told, but also to process and really engage with that information so that we can also return it to the speaker if appropriate.
- There are six increasing levels of listening: passive, responsive, selective, attentive,

active, and empathic. Remember your role as a listener with the HUR acronym: **h**ear the message, **u**nderstand it, and **r**espond. We can respond and show our understanding by paraphrasing, reflecting, and summarizing.

CHAPTER 4. AS IF IT WASN'T HARD ENOUGH...

- The goal during conflict is to increase positive feelings for everyone involved. One way to do this is with Carroll's COIN framework—context, observations, impact, and next (follow-up actions). Use plenty of "I" statements, pause often, and be as clear and direct as possible. When giving feedback, focus on what can be done in the future rather than what has already been done.
- There are many ways to navigate communication when you disagree. The agreement frame helps the other person release their resistance to your perspective because you are able to really support *their* views or values first and seek common ground that puts you on the same team.
- The art of saying no includes understanding the different kinds of assertions, including

basic assertions (statements of facts and limits), empathic assertions (asserting needs and limits whilst acknowledging others' with kindness), consequence assertions (following through with consequences of not respecting your boundary), discrepancy assertions (drawing attention to difference between what was agreed and what is happening), and negative feeling assertions (owning your own emotions and stating them).
- VOMP is another technique and stands for voice/vent, own, moccasins, and plan. Say your piece and allow the other person to say theirs, own your part in the conflict, show empathy for their perspective, and then move forward with a concrete plan on how to act in the future.
- Marshall Rosenberg's nonviolent communication is about making neutral observations, expressing feelings with "I" statements, sharing needs, and making reasonable and respectful requests.
- If none of these three techniques work, you can manage a difficult person by "fogging" (being as neutral and non-reactive as possible) or repeating boundaries like a "broken record" until they lose interest.
- Finally, learn the six elements of a successful and genuine apology: express regret and remorse, explain yourself, accept full responsibility, repent, make an offer for

reparations, and, only at the end, request forgiveness. Realize that you are not entitled to forgiveness, and accept whatever happens with grace.

CHAPTER 5. GOAL-ORIENTED COMMUNICATION

- Persuasion is about trying to change or influence someone's mind, and it rests on knowing what that person's values, perspectives, and needs are so you can address them directly.
- According to Aristotle, the four main modes of persuasion are ethos (appeal to authority), pathos (appeal to emotion), logos (appeal to reason), and kairos (making an argument at the right time and place). Good oration and rhetoric are not about which mode fits you or your message best, but knowing how to put your message in a form that the audience is most likely to hear.
- To speak to pathos, be vulnerable or share a personal experience or even a secret. To speak to logos, use hard data and evidence or a deductive or inductive argument. To speak to ethos, share genuine and relevant credentials. In all cases, try to understand your audience's emotional state, their perspective, and their most pressing need,

- then present your message in terms that will appeal to them most.
- Workplace communication runs on all the same communication rules, but we have to consider the bigger role that written and electronic communication plays, too. Professional communication is more about appropriateness, politeness, custom, convention, and formality.
- We need to consider the goal, content, and medium to the message, as well as the audience. First, clarify the reason for communication and let that decide the most appropriate medium. Factor in your company's unique communication culture and be mindful of your tone.
- Professional communication should follow the seven Cs: It should be clear, concise, correct, concrete, considerate, complete, and courteous.

www.ingramcontent.com/pod-product-compliance
Lightning Source LLC
Chambersburg PA
CBHW060600080526
44585CB00013B/641